Reading Schedule

이 책은 총 31,000여개의 단어로 구성되어 있습니다.(중복 포함, 1페이지는 대략 147단어)
분당 150단어 읽기는 원어민이 말하는 속도입니다. 먼저 이 기준을 목표로 시작해보세요.

● 1회 읽기

날 짜	/	/	/	/	/
시 간	~	~	~	~	~
페이지	~	~	~	~	~

내용 이해도　✓ 90%이상　　✓ 70%　　✓ 50%　　✓ 30%이하

리딩속도 계산　　212　÷　　　　　×　147　=

　　　　　　　전체 페이지　　　시간(분)　　1페이지 당 평균 단어수　분당 읽은 단어수

● 2회 읽기

날 짜	/	/	/	/	/
시 간	~	~	~	~	~
페이지	~	~	~	~	~

내용 이해도　✓ 90%이상　　✓ 70%　　✓ 50%　　✓ 30%이하

리딩속도 계산　　212　÷　　　　　×　147　=

　　　　　　　전체 페이지　　　시간(분)　　1페이지 당 평균 단어수　분당 읽은 단어수

● 3회 읽기

날 짜	/	/	/	/	/
시 간	~	~	~	~	~
페이지	~	~	~	~	~

내용 이해도　✓ 90%이상　　✓ 70%　　✓ 50%　　✓ 30%이하

리딩속도 계산　　212　÷　　　　　×　147　=

　　　　　　　전체 페이지　　　시간(분)　　1페이지 당 평균 단어수　분당 읽은 단어수

식은 죽
먹기야~

● 전체 평가

체감 난이도 　☑ 상 　☑ 상중 　☑ 중 　☑ 중하 　☑ 하

읽기 만족도 　☑ 나는 리딩의 고수!

　　　　　　☑ 좀 잘했군요~

　　　　　　☑ 노력하세요.

　　　　　　☑ 난 머리가 안 좋나봐 -.-;

플랜더스의 개

리딩 속도가 빨라지는 영어책 014

플랜더스의 개
A DOG OF FLANDERS

2020년 10월 10일 초판 1쇄 인쇄
2020년 10월 15일 초판 1쇄 발행

지은이 위다
발행인 손건
편집기획 김상배
마케팅 이언영
디자인 이성세
제작 최승용
인쇄 선경프린테크

발행처 LanCom 랭컴
주소 서울시 금천구 시흥대로193, 709호
등록번호 제 312-2006-00060호
전화 02) 2636-0895
팩스 02) 2636-0896
홈페이지 www.lancom.co.kr

ISBN 979-11-89204-71-6 13740

플랜더스의 개

A DOG OF FLANDERS

뉘른베르크의 난로

THE NÜRNBERG STOVE

위다 지음

LanCom
Language & Communication

CONTENTS

플랜더스의 개

A DOG OF FLANDERS

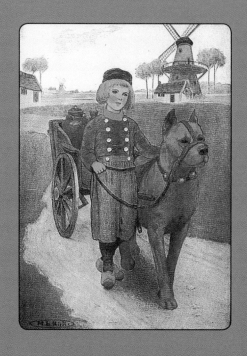

A DOG OF FLANDERS

Nello and Patrasche were left all alone in
남겨지다 홀로; 혼자서, 외로이
the world.
세계, 세상, 지구
They were friends in a friendship closer than
친구 우정, 친선 더 가까운
brotherhood. Nello was a little Ardennois, Pa-
인류애, 형제애 아르텐 태생[출신]의 사람
trasche was a big Fleming. They were both of
플랜더스 출신[태생]의 사람 둘 다
the same age by length of years, yet one was still
같은 나이, 동갑 길이, 시간, 기간 해, 연[년] 아직(도)
young, and the other was already old.
이미, 벌써
They had dwelt together almost all their
(…에) 살다[거주하다](dwell)
days: both were orphaned and destitute, and
고아로 만들다 극빈한, 궁핍한
owed their lives to the same hand.
신세를 지고 있다
It had been the beginning of the tie between
초(반), 시작 (강한) 유대[관계]
them, their first bond of sympathy; and it had
유대, 끈 동정, 연민; 공감
strengthened day by day, and had grown with
강화되다, 강력해지다 나날이, 하루하루, 날이 갈수록

their growth, firm and indissoluble, until they
성장, 증가　딱딱한, 단단한　서로 떼어놓을 수 없는, 불가분의

loved one another very greatly.
서로(서로)

Their home was a little hut on the edge of
오두막, 막사　끝, 가장자리

a little village, a Flemish village a league from
(시골) 마을, 부락, 촌락　플랜더스 마을　거리의 단위; 약 3마일

Antwerp, set amidst flat breadths of pasture and
앤트워프(벨기에의 항구 도시)　평평한　폭넓음　초원, 목초지

corn-lands, with long lines of poplars and of
옥수수밭　포플러나무

alders bending in the breeze on the edge of the
오리나무　굽히다, 숙이다　산들바람, 미풍

great canal which ran through it.
운하, 수로

It had about a score of houses and home-
20, 스무 개 정도　농가 (주택)

steads, with shutters of bright green or sky-blue,
덧문, 셔터　밝은, 빛나는 초록색　하늘색

and roofs rose-red or black and white, and walls
지붕　빨간 장밋빛　검은색　하얀색　벽, 담

white-washed until they shone in the sun like
백색 도료, 회반죽　빛나다(shine)　~처럼

snow.
눈

In the centre of the village stood a windmill,
중심, 중앙, 가운데　풍차

placed on a little moss-grown slope: it was a
놓다, 두다, 자리하다　이끼가 낀; 고풍스러운　(산)비탈, 경사면

landmark to all the level country round.
주요 지형지물, 랜드마크　평평한; (높이·위치·가치 등이) 같은[대등한]

It had once been painted scarlet, sails and
한때　진홍색, 다홍색　(풍차의) 날개

all, but that had been in its infancy, half a cen-
(발달의) 초창기[초기]

tury or more earlier, when it had ground wheat
앞서, 먼저　밀을 빻다

for the soldiers of Napoleon; and it was now a
군인, 군대　나폴레옹　이제, 지금

ruddy brown, tanned by wind and weather.
불그레한　갈색　햇볕에 타다[그을리다]　바람　날씨, 기상

It went queerly by fits and starts, as though
기묘하게, 이상하게 간헐적으로; 하다가 말다가[단속적으로]

rheumatic and stiff in the joints from age, but
류머티즘 (환자) 뻣뻣한, 뻑뻑한 관절

it served the whole neighborhood, which would
전체[전부]의, 모든, 온전한 이웃(사람들)

have thought it almost as impious to carry grain
불경한, 불경스러운, 신의가 없는

elsewhere as to attend any other religious ser-
(어딘가) 다른 곳에서[으로] 참석하다; (…에) 다니다 종교의

vice than the mass that was performed at the
수행하다, 실시하다

altar of the little old gray church, with its conical
회색 교회, 성당 원뿔 모양의

steeple, which stood opposite to it, and whose
(교회의) 첨탑 … 맞은편의

single bell rang morning, noon, and night with
울리다(ring)

that strange, subdued, hollow sadness which ev-
낯선, 이상한 가라앉은; 은은한 공허한 슬픔

ery bell that hangs in the Low Countries seems
저지대 국가(벨기에, 네덜란드 등 지대가 낮은)

to gain as an integral part of its melody.
필수적인, 필요불가결한

Within sound of the little melancholy clock
구슬픈, 우울한

almost from their birth upward, they had dwelt
거의, 대부분 탄생, 출생 살다, 거주하다

together, Nello and Patrasche, in the little
함께

hut on the edge of the village, with the cathe-
오두막 끝, 가장자리 대성당

dral spire of Antwerp rising in the north-east,
첨탑 북동쪽

beyond the great green plain of seeding grass
…저편에[너머] 평원, 평지; 들판 씨앗을 뿌린

and spreading corn that stretched away from
펼쳐진 길게 뻗은[펼쳐져 있는]

them like a tideless, changeless sea.
조수의 간만이 없는 변화 없는, 변하지 않는

It was the hut of a very old man, of a very
오두막, 막사   매우, 대단히

poor man--of old Jehan Daas, who in his time
가난한, 빈곤한

had been a soldier, and who remembered the
군인   기억하다

wars that had trampled the country as oxen
전쟁   짓밟다, 밟아 뭉개다   나라, 국가   OX의 복수

tread down the furrows, and who had brought
밟아서 뭉개다[으깨다](=trample) 고랑, 골

from his service nothing except a wound, which
(누구·무엇을) 제외하고는[외에는]

had made him a cripple.
불구자

When old Jehan Daas had reached his full
닿다, 도달하다

eighty, his daughter had died in the Ardennes,
80   딸   죽다

hard by Stavelot, and had left him in legacy her
스타벨로 근처에서   (죽은 사람이 남긴) 유산

two-year-old son.
두 살 먹은   아들

The old man could ill contrive to support
용케[어떻게든] …하다 부양하다, 먹이다

himself, but he took up the additional burden
추가의(=extra)   부담, 짐

uncomplainingly, and it soon became welcome
불평 없이, 불평하지 않고   곧, 금방

and precious to him.
귀중한, 소중한

Little Nello--which was but a pet diminutive
약칭

for Nicolas--throve with him, and the old man
번창하다, 잘 자라다(thrive)

and the little child lived in the poor little hut
어린이, 아이   가난한, 초라한, 빈약한

contentedly.
만족스럽게, 기꺼이.

It was a very humble little mud-hut indeed,
변변치 않은, 초라한　　흙집　　　　정말로, 참으로

but it was clean and white as a sea-shell, and
깨끗한, 깔끔한　　　　　조개껍질

stood in a small plot of garden-ground that
정원용 땅

yielded beans and herbs and pumpkins.
농작물을 내다[생산하다]　　허브　　　호박

They were very poor, terribly poor--many a
가난한　　끔찍하게, 참혹하게

day they had nothing at all to eat. They never by
아무것도　　전혀　　먹다

any chance had enough: to have had enough to
충분히 먹다

eat would have been to have reached paradise
닿다, 도착하다　　천국, 낙원

at once.
즉시[당장/지체 없이]

But the old man was very gentle and good to
온화한, 순한; 조용한, 조심스러운

the boy, and the boy was a beautiful, innocent,
아름다운　　　　순수한

truthful, tender-hearted creature; and they were
진실한　　마음씨 고운, 인정 많은　　존재, 생명체

happy on a crust and a few leaves of cabbage,
행복한　　(빵) 껍질[조각]　　　　잎사귀　　양배추

and asked no more of earth or heaven; save
요청하다　　　　땅, 지구　　하늘, 천국

indeed that Patrasche should be always with
늘, 항상

them, since without Patrasche where would they
~없이

have been?

For Patrasche was their alpha and omega;
(…의) 처음과 끝, 전체(of)

their treasury and granary; their store of gold
보물　　　　곡물 저장고, 곡창　　저장고

and wand of wealth; their bread-winner and
요술지팡이　　(많은) 재산　　(집안의) 생계비를 버는 사람, 가장

minister; their only friend and comforter.
장관, 각료　　　　유일한, 하나뿐인　　위안을 주는[위로가 되는] 사람

Patrasche dead or gone from them, they
must have laid themselves down and died likewise. Patrasche was body, brains, hands, head,
and feet to both of them: Patrasche was their
very life, their very soul. For Jehan Daas was old
and a cripple, and Nello was but a child; and Patrasche was their dog.

A dog of Flanders--yellow of hide, large of
head and limb, with wolf-like ears that stood
erect, and legs bowed and feet widened in the
muscular development wrought in his breed by
many generations of hard service.

Patrasche came of a race which had toiled
hard and cruelly from sire to son in Flanders
many a century--slaves of slaves, dogs of the
people, beasts of the shafts and the harness,
creatures that lived straining their sinews in the
gall of the cart, and died breaking their hearts
on the flints of the streets.

Patrasche had been born of parents who had labored hard all their days over the sharp-set stones of the various cities and the long, shadowless, weary roads of the two Flanders and of Brabant.

He had been born to no other heritage than those of pain and of toil. He had been fed on curses and baptized with blows.

Why not? It was a Christian country, and Patrasche was but a dog.

Before he was fully grown he had known the bitter gall of the cart and the collar. Before he had entered his thirteenth month he had become the property of a hardware-dealer, who was accustomed to wander over the land north and south, from the blue sea to the green mountains.

They sold him for a small price, because he was so young. This man was a drunkard and a brute. The life of Patrasche was a life of hell. To deal the tortures of hell on the animal creation

14

is a way which the Christians have of showing their belief in it.

His purchaser was a sullen, ill-living, brutal Brabantois, who heaped his cart full with pots and pans and flagons and buckets, and other wares of crockery and brass and tin, and left Patrasche to draw the load as best he might, whilst he himself lounged idly by the side in fat and sluggish ease, smoking his black pipe and stopping at every wineshop or cafe on the road.

Happily for Patrasche--or unhappily--he was very strong: he came of an iron race, long born and bred to such cruel travail; so that he did not die, but managed to drag on a wretched existence under the brutal burdens, the scarifying lashes, the hunger, the thirst, the blows, the curses, and the exhaustion which are the only wages with which the Flemings repay the most patient and laborious of all their four-footed victims.

One day, after two years of this long and
~뒤에 2년 긴

deadly agony, Patrasche was going on as usual
죽을 지경의 극도의 (육체적·정신적) 고통[괴로움] 늘 그렇듯이

along one of the straight, dusty, unlovely roads
~을 따라 곧은, 똑바른 먼지투성이의

that lead to the city of Rubens.

It was full midsummer, and very warm. His
한여름 더운

cart was very heavy, piled high with goods in
무거운 (물건을 차곡차곡) 쌓다[포개다]

metal and in earthenware.
금속, 철물 도기, 토기, 옹기, 사기

His owner sauntered on without noticing
한가로이[느긋하게] 걷다 (=stroll)

him otherwise than by the crack of the whip as
그 외에는 채찍을 휘두르다

it curled round his quivering loins. The Braban-
떨리는, 떨고 있는 허리, 요부

tois had paused to drink beer himself at every
잠시 멈추다 마시다 맥주

wayside house, but he had forbidden Patrasche
길가, 도로변 금(지)하다, ~을 못하게 하다

to stop a moment for a draught from the canal.
멈추다 죽 들이마시기, 한 모금 운하, 수로

Going along thus, in the full sun, on a
이렇게 하여, 이와 같이

scorching highway, having eaten nothing for
작열하는, 뜨겁게 달궈진

twenty-four hours, and, which was far worse to
24시간

him, not having tasted water for near twelve,
맛보다 물 거의, ~가까이

being blind with dust, sore with blows, and stu-

pefied with the merciless weight which dragged
무자비한, 인정사정없는

upon his loins, Patrasche staggered and foamed
비틀[휘청]거리며 가다 입에 거품을 물다

a little at the mouth, and fell.
넘어지다, 쓰러지다(fall)

He fell in the middle of the white, dusty
가운데 먼지 나는
road, in the full glare of the sun; he was sick
환한 빛, 눈부심 아픈
unto death, and motionless.
…(때)까지 움직이지 않는, 가만히 있는
His master gave him the only medicine in
오직 약
his pharmacy--kicks and oaths and blows with
약국 발로 차기 욕설 매질, 구타
a cudgel of oak, which had been often the only
곤봉, 몽둥이 오크나무, 떡갈나무, 참나무 자주, 흔히
food and drink, the only wage and reward, ever
먹이 음료 급료 보상
offered to him.
제공하다
But Patrasche was beyond the reach of any
~뒤에, ~너머 도착, 도달
torture or of any curses.
고문 욕설, 저주
Patrasche lay, dead to all appearances, down
등장, 출연; 출두
in the white powder of the summer dust.
하얀 가루
After a while, finding it useless to assail his
알다, 깨닫다 소용없는 공격하다; 괴롭히다
ribs with punishment and his ears with maledic-
갈비(뼈), 늑골 벌, 처벌, 형벌 저주, 악담, 욕
tions, the Brabantois--deeming life gone in him,
(…로) 여기다[생각하다]
or going so nearly that his carcass was forever
(큰 동물의) 시체, 죽은 동물
useless, unless indeed some one should strip
…하지 않는 한, …이 아닌 한 벗기다
it of the skin for gloves--cursed him fiercely in
피부, 가죽 장갑 사납게, 맹렬하게
farewell, struck off the leathern bands of the
작별, 이별 가죽으로 만든
harness, kicked his body aside into the grass,
마구 한쪽으로, (길을) 비켜
and, groaning and muttering in savage wrath,
신음[끙 하는] 소리를 내다 투덜거리다, 불평하다 맹렬한, 사나운 분노, 노여움

pushed the cart lazily along the road up-hill, and left the dying dog for the ants to sting and for the crows to pick.

It was the last day before Kermesse away at Louvain, and the Brabantois was in haste to reach the fair and get a good place for his truck of brass wares.

He was in fierce wrath, because Patrasche had been a strong and much-enduring animal, and because he himself had now the hard task of pushing his charette all the way to Louvain. But to stay to look after Patrasche never en-tered his thoughts: the beast was dying and use-less, and he would steal, to replace him, the first large dog that he found wandering alone out of sight of its master.

Patrasche had cost him nothing, or next to nothing, and for two long, cruel years had made him toil ceaselessly in his service from sunrise to sunset, through summer and winter, in fair weather and foul.

He had got a fair use and a good profit out
of Patrasche: being human, he was wise, and
left the dog to draw his last breath alone in the
ditch, and have his bloodshot eyes plucked out
as they might be by the birds, whilst he himself
went on his way to beg and to steal, to eat and to
drink, to dance and to sing, in the mirth at Louvain.

A dying dog, a dog of the cart--why should
he waste hours over its agonies at peril of losing
a handful of copper coins, at peril of a shout of
laughter?

Patrasche lay there, flung in the grass-green
ditch. It was a busy road that day, and hundreds
of people, on foot and on mules, in wagons or in
carts, went by, tramping quickly and joyously
on to Louvain.

Some saw him, most did not even look: all
passed on. A dead dog more or less--it was nothing in Brabant: it would be nothing anywhere in
the world.

After a time, among the holiday-makers, there came a little old man who was bent and lame, and very feeble. He was in no guise for feasting: he was very poorly and miserably clad, and he dragged his silent way slowly through the dust among the pleasure-seekers.

He looked at Patrasche, paused, wondered, turned aside, then kneeled down in the rank grass and weeds of the ditch, and surveyed the dog with kindly eyes of pity.

There was with him a little rosy, fair-haired, dark-eyed child of a few years old, who pattered in amidst the bushes, for him breast-high, and stood gazing with a pretty seriousness upon the poor, great, quiet beast.

Thus it was that these two first met--the little Nello and the big Patrasche.

The upshot of that day was, that old Jehan Daas, with much laborious effort, drew the sufferer homeward to his own little hut, which was a stone's throw off amidst the fields, and there

20

tended him with so much care that the sickness, which had been a brain seizure, brought on by heat and thirst and exhaustion, with time and shade and rest passed away, and health and strength returned, and Patrasche staggered up again upon his four stout, tawny legs.

Now for many weeks he had been useless, powerless, sore, near to death; but all this time he had heard no rough word, had felt no harsh touch, but only the pitying murmurs of the child's voice and the soothing caress of the old man's hand.

In his sickness they too had grown to care for him, this lonely man and the little happy child. He had a corner of the hut, with a heap of dry grass for his bed; and they had learned to listen eagerly for his breathing in the dark night, to tell them that he lived; and when he first was well enough to essay a loud, hollow, broken bay, they laughed aloud, and almost wept together for joy at such a sign of his sure restoration; and little Nello, in delighted glee (아주 기뻐하는), hung round his (신이 남) ruggcd neck (강인하게[다부지게] 생긴) with chains of marguerites (마거리트 꽃), and kissed him with fresh and ruddy lips (신선한, 싱싱한 / (색깔이) 붉은, 불그스름한).

So then, when Patrasche arose (일어나다(arise)), himself again, strong, big, gaunt (수척한, 아주 여윈), powerful (강한, 힘센 / 큰), his great wistful eyes (애석해[아쉬워]하는) had a gentle astonishment (깜짝[크게] 놀람(=amazement)) in them that there were no curses (욕(설), 악담) to rouse him and no blows to drive him; and his heart awakened to ((감정이) 일다[일깨워지다]) a mighty love (강력한, 힘센), which never wavered ((불안하게) 흔들리다) once in its fidelity (충실함, 신의) whilst life abode (머무르다, 깃들이다(abide)) with him.

But Patrasche, being a dog, was grateful (고마워하는, 감사하는). Patrasche lay pondering (숙고하다, 곰곰이 생각하다 (=consider)) long with grave, tender, musing brown eyes (사색하다, 골똘히 생각하다(=ponder)), watching the movements of (움직임) his friends (친구).

Now, the old soldier (군인), Jehan Daas, could do nothing for his living but limp about a little (다리를 절다[절뚝거리다]) with a small cart (작은 / 손수레), with which he carried daily (운반하다, 나르다) the milk-cans (우유통) of those happier neighbors who (이웃(사람)) owned cattle ((집합적으로) 소) away into the town of Antwerp ((도시(city)보다 작은) (소)도시, 읍). The villagers (마을 사람) gave him the employment (직장; 취업, 고용, 채용) a little out of charity (자선; 너그러움, 관용)--more because it suited them ((…에게) 편리하다[맞다])

well to send their milk into the town by so honest a carrier, and bide at home themselves to
look after their gardens, their cows, their poul-
try, or their little fields.

But it was becoming hard work for the old
man. He was eighty-three, and Antwerp was a
good league off, or more.

Patrasche watched the milk-cans come and
go that one day when he had got well and was

lying in the sun with the wreath of marguerites
round his tawny neck.

The next morning, Patrasche, before the old
man had touched the cart, arose and walked to
it and placed himself betwixt its handles, and
testified as plainly as dumb show could do his
desire and his ability to work in return for the
bread of charity that he had eaten.

Jehan Daas resisted long, for the old man
was one of those who thought it a foul shame
to bind dogs to labor for which Nature never
formed them.

But Patrasche would not be gainsaid: finding
부정하다, 반대하다(gainsay)

they did not harness him, he tried to draw the
마구   시도하다

cart onward with his teeth.
앞으로[계속 이어서] 나아가는

At length Jehan Daas gave way, vanquished
한참 있다가   완파하다(=conquer)

by the persistence and the gratitude of this crea-
고집. (오래 동안) 지속됨   고마움, 감사, 사의

ture whom he had succored. He fashioned his
원조하다, 구조하다   (손으로) 만들다

cart so that Patrasche could run in it, and this he

did every morning of his life thenceforward.
매, 모든   그 때부터

When the winter came, Jehan Daas thanked
겨울   감사하다

the blessed fortune that had brought him to the
복 받은, 축복된   행운   가져오다

dying dog in the ditch that fair-day of Louvain;
죽어가는   도랑

for he was very old, and he grew feebler with
아주 약한

each year, and he would ill have known how to
각각[각자](의)   병들다

pull his load of milk-cans over the snows and
끌다   짐   우유통   눈

through the deep ruts in the mud if it had not
깊은   바퀴 자국   진흙

been for the strength and the industry of the
근면한, 부지런한

animal he had befriended.
(도움이 필요한 사람에게) 친구가 되어 주다

As for Patrasche, it seemed heaven to him.
천국, 하늘나라

After the frightful burdens that his old master
끔찍한   (운반하기 힘든) 짐

had compelled him to strain under, at the call of
강요하다, 강제하다   (근육 등을) 혹사하다[무리하게 사용하다]

the whip at every step, it seemed nothing to him
채찍

but amusement to step out with this little light
green cart, with its bright brass cans, by the side
of the gentle old man who always paid him with
a tender caress and with a kindly word.

Besides, his work was over by three or four
in the day, and after that time he was free to do
as he would--to stretch himself, to sleep in the
sun, to wander in the fields, to romp with the
young child, or to play with his fellow-dogs. Patrasche was very happy.

Fortunately for his peace, his former owner
was killed in a drunken brawl at the Kermesse
of Mechlin, and so sought not after him nor
disturbed him in his new and well-loved home.

A few years later, old Jehan Daas, who had always been a cripple, became so paralyzed with rheumatism that it was impossible for him to go out with the cart any more.

Then little Nello, being now grown to his sixth year of age, and knowing the town well from having accompanied his grandfather so many times, took his place beside the cart, and sold the milk and received the coins in exchange, and brought them back to their respective owners with a pretty grace and seriousness which charmed all who beheld him.

The little Ardennois was a beautiful child, with dark, grave, tender eyes, and a lovely bloom upon his face, and fair locks that clustered to his throat; and many an artist sketched the group as it went by him--the green cart with the brass flagons of Teniers and Mieris and Van Tal, and the great tawny-colored, massive dog, with his belled harness that chimed cheerily as he went, and the small figure that ran beside him which

had little white feet in great wooden shoes, and
a soft, grave, innocent, happy face like the little
fair children of Rubens.

나무로 만든 신발 / 부드러운 진지한 순진한, 순수한 행복한 / 루벤스(1577-1640) (플랜더스의 화가)

Nello and Patrasche did the work so well
and so joyfully together that Jehan Daas himself, when the summer came and he was better
again, had no need to stir out, but could sit in
the doorway in the sun and see them go forth
through the garden wicket, and then doze and
dream and pray a little, and then awakc again as
the clock tolled three and watch for their return.

무척 즐겁게 / 좋아지다, 나아지다 / (…을) 필요로 하다, (반드시) …해야 하다 / 출입구, 문간 …쪽으로 / 쪽문, 작은문 깜빡 잠이 들다, 졸다 / 꿈을 꾸다 기도하다 (잠에서) 깨나 / <종·시계가> 치다, <시각을> 알리다 귀환, 돌아옴

And on their return Patrasche would shake
himself free of his harness with a bay of glee,
and Nello would recount with pride the doings
of the day; and they would all go in together to
their meal of rye bread and milk or soup, and
would see the shadows lengthen over the great
plain, and see the twilight veil the fair cathedral
spire; and then lie down together to sleep peace-
fully while the old man said a prayer.

털다, 흔들다 / 마구 으르렁거림 신이 남 / (경험한 것에 대해) 이야기하다 / 식사, 끼니, 밥 호밀 빵 우유 수프 / 그림자 길어지다, 늘어나다; 길게 하다, 늘이다 / 황혼, 땅거미 (얇은 막 같은 것이) 가리다 / 평화롭게 / 기도문, 기도(내용)

So the days and the years went on, and the lives of Nello (삶, 생(명)) and Patrasche were happy (행복한), innocent (순수한), and healthful (건강한, 강건한).

In the spring (봄) and summer (여름) especially (특별히, 특히) were they glad (기쁜, 반가운, 고마운). Flanders is not a lovely (사랑스러운, 아름다운, 매력적인) land, and around the burgh (자치구, 자치 도시) of Rubens it is perhaps (어쩌면, 아마도) least lovely of all.

Corn and colza (옥수수 / 유채), pasture (목초지, 초원) and plough (경작지, 논밭), succeed each other (서로) on the characterless (특징 없는) plain (평원, 들판) in wearying (지겨운) repetition (반복, 되풀이]), and save by some gaunt gray (삭막한) tower, with its peal of pathetic (불쌍한, 애처로운) bells, or some figure coming athwart (가로질러) the fields, made picturesque (그림 같은(특히 고풍스러운)) by a gleaner's (이삭줍는 사람, 수집가) bundle or a woodman's (나무꾼) fagot (장작뭇[단], 삭정이단), there is no change (변화), no variety (다양성, 다채로움), no beauty (아름다움) anywhere; and he who has dwelt (살다, 거주하다(dwell의 과거·과거분사)) upon the mountains or amidst the forests (숲, 삼림) feels oppressed (압박감을 주다, 우울하게 만들다) as by imprisonment with the tedium (지루함 (=boredom)) and the endlessness (끝없음, 무한함, 영원함) of that vast (어마어마한) and dreary (음울한, 따분한 (=dull)) level.

But it is green and very fertile, and it has wide horizons that have a certain charm of their own even in their dulness and monotony; and among the rushes by the water-side the flowers grow, and the trees rise tall and fresh where the barges glide with their great hulks black against the sun, and their little green barrels and vari-colored flags gay against the leaves.

Anyway, there is greenery and breadth of space enough to be as good as beauty to a child and a dog; and these two asked no better, when their work was done, than to lie buried in the lush grasses on the side of the canal, and watch the cumbrous vessels drifting by and bring the crisp salt smell of the sea among the blossoming scents of the country summer.

True, in the winter it was harder, and they had to rise in the darkness and the bitter cold, and they had seldom as much as they could have eaten any day, and the hut was scarce better than a shed when the nights were cold, although

30

it looked so pretty in warm weather, buried in
예쁜 　따스한 　날씨

a great kindly clambering vine, that never bore
어오르다, 기어 가다 포도 넝쿨 　낳다, 생산하다

fruit, indeed, but which covered it with luxuri-
과일, 열매 정말로, 실제로 　화려한

ant green tracery all through the months of
(직선과 곡선으로 된) 장식 무늬 　달, 월, 개월

blossom and harvest.
꽃 　추수, 수확

　　In winter the winds found many holes in
바람 　많은 　구멍

the walls of the poor little hut, and the vine was
벽, 담 　가난한, 초라한 　포도넝쿨

black and leafless, and the bare lands looked
검은색 　잎이 없는[떨어진](=bare)

very bleak and drear without, and sometimes
황량한, 음산한 음울한, 따분한(=dull) 　가끔, 때때로

within the floor was flooded and then frozen.
마루, 바닥 물에 잠기다, 침수되다 얼어붙다

　　In winter it was hard, and the snow numbed
(추위 등으로) 감각이 없는

the little white limbs of Nello, and the icicles cut
팔다리 　얼음조각

the brave, untiring feet of Patrasche.
용감한 지치지 않는

　　But even then they were never heard to

lament, either of them. The child's wooden
한탄하다, 통탄하다 　나막신

shoes and the dog's four legs would trot man-
빨리 걷다, 속보로 가다

fully together over the frozen fields to the chime
얼어붙은 　벨을 울리다

of the bells on the harness; and then sometimes,
마구 　가끔, 때때로

in the streets of Antwerp, some housewife
거리, 길, 도로 　주부

would bring them a bowl of soup and a hand-
가져다주다 　그릇, 사발

ful of bread, or some kindly trader would throw
상인, 거래자

some billets of fuel into the little cart as it went
굵은 막대기, 장작개비, 짧은 통나무

homeward, or some woman in their own village
집으로

would bid them keep a share of the milk they
몫, 지분

carried for their own food; and they would run
실어 나르다[전달하다]   음식   달리다

over the white lands, through the early dark-
땅   일찍

ness, bright and happy, and burst with a shout
밝은, 빛나는   행복한   터뜨리다, 파열시키다

of joy into their home.
기쁨, 즐거움

So, on the whole, it was well with them, very
전체[전반]적으로 보아, 대체로   잘, 좋게, 제대로

well; and Patrasche, meeting on the highway or
만나다   고속도로, 공공 도로

in the public streets the many dogs who toiled
공공의, 일반의 거리, 도로   힘들게 일하다

from daybreak into nightfall, paid only with
새벽   밤중

blows and curses, and loosened from the shafts
매질, 구타   욕설, 저주   풀다, 늦추다   (마차수레의) 끌채

with a kick to starve and freeze as best they
발길질   굶주림   얼다, 얼리다

might-- Patrasche in his heart was very grate-
진심으로   감사하다, 고마워하다

ful to his fate, and thought it the fairest and the
운명, 숙명   가장 공정한, 가장 멋진[좋은]

kindliest the world could hold.

Though he was often very hungry indeed
비록 ~일지라도   자주, 흔히   굶주리다

when he lay down at night; though he had to

work in the heats of summer noons and the
일하다   열기   여름

rasping chills of winter dawns; though his feet
살을 에는 냉기, 한기   새벽, 동틀녘

were often tender with wounds from the sharp
부드러운   부상   날카로운

edges of the jagged pavement; though he had to
끝, 가장자리   삐죽삐죽한, 들쭉날쭉한

perform tasks beyond his strength and against
임무, 과업

his nature--yet he was grateful and content: he
본성, 천성   감사하다   만족하다

did his duty with each day, and the eyes that he
임무, 의무

loved smiled down on him. It was sufficient for
미소짓는   충분한, 족한, 넉넉한

Patrasche.

There was only one thing which caused Pa-
오직, 단지   야기하다, 발생시키다

trasche any uneasiness in his life, and it was this.
불안, 걱정, 불쾌; 거북함

Antwerp, as all the world knows, is full at every
세상이 다 알듯이, 누구나 다 아는 것처럼

turn of old piles of stones, dark and ancient and
(위로 차곡차곡) 포개[쌓아] 놓은 것, 더미   아주 오래된

majestic, standing in crooked courts, jammed
장엄한, 위풍당당한   비뚤어진, 구부러진

against gateways and taverns, rising by the wa-
(문이 달려 있는) 입구   퍼브(pub), 여관

ter's edge, with bells ringing above them in the
울리는

air, and ever and again out of their arched doors
허공, 공기   아치형 문

a swell of music pealing.
붓다, 부풀다   종소리; (울리듯 이어지는) 큰 소리

There they remain, the grand old sanctuaries
남다, 남아 있다   웅장한, 장려한   피난처, 안식처

of the past, shut in amidst the squalor, the
과거, 지난날   불결한[누추한] 상태

hurry, the crowds, the unloveliness, and the
군중   예쁘지 않음, 못생김.

commerce of the modern world, and all day
무역, 상업   현대적인, 모던한

long the clouds drift and the birds circle and the
구름   흘러가다, 떠가다   (공중에서) 빙빙 돌다

winds sigh around them, and beneath the earth
한숨 쉬나   ~아래[밑]에

at their feet there sleeps--RUBENS.

foot의 복수

And the greatness of the mighty Master still

위대함 / 강력한, 힘센 / 주인, 스승

rests upon Antwerp, and wherever we turn in its

narrow streets his glory lies therein, so that all

좁은, 가는 / 길, 거리 / 영광, 영예 / 그 안에

mean things are thereby transfigured; and as we

(더 아름답게) 변모시키다

pace slowly through the winding ways, and by

서성거리다 / 구불구불한

the edge of the stagnant water, and through the

고여 있는

noisome courts, his spirit abides with us, and

(극도로) 역겨운[고약한] / 정신, 영혼 / 머무르다, 깃들이다

the heroic beauty of his visions is about us, and

영웅적인 / 아름다움 / 시력, 눈; 시야

the stones that once felt his footsteps and bore

돌 / 한때 / 발자국

his shadow seem to arise and speak of him with

그림자 / 깨어나다

living voices.

살아있는, 생생한

For the city which is the tomb of Rubens still

도시 / 무덤

lives to us through him, and him alone.

It is so quiet there by that great white sepul-

조용한, 고요한 / 거대한 / 돌로 만든) 무덤[매장지]

chre--so quiet, save only when the organ peals

크게 울리다

and the choir cries aloud the Salve Regina or the

합창단, 성가대 / 살베 레지나(경하합니다, 마리아여)

Kyrie Eleison. Sure no artist ever had a greater

화가, 예술가

gravestone than that pure marble sanctuary

묘비; 돌무덤 / 순수한 / 대리석 / 성소, 성역

gives to him in the heart of his birthplace in the

생가, 출생지

chancel of St. Jacques.

성단소(교회 예배 때 성직자와 합창대가 앉는 제단 옆 자리)

Without Rubens(~없이), what were Antwerp? A dirty(더러운), dusky(어스름한, 칙칙한), bustling(부산한, 북적거리는) mart, which no man would ever care to look upon save the traders(상인) who do business on its wharves(부두, 선창(wharf의 복수)).

With Rubens, to the whole(전체[전부]의, 모든, 온전한) world of men it is a sacred(성스러운, 종교적인, 신성시되는) name, a sacred soil, a Bethlehem(국가, 국토, 땅) where a god of Art(예술) saw light, a Golgotha(골고다) where a god of Art lies dead.

O nations(국가; (한 국가의 전체) 국민)! closely should you treasure(보물) your great(위대한) men, for by them alone will the future(미래, 장래) know of you.

Flanders in her generations(세대, 대(약 30년을 단위로 하는 시대 구분)) has been wise. In his life she glorified(미화하다, 영광되게 하다, 찬미하다) this greatest of her sons, and in his death she magnifies(확대하다, 과장하다) his name. But her wisdom(지혜, 현명함) is very rare(드문, 보기 힘든, 희귀한).

Now, the trouble(애, 문제, 곤란, 골칫거리) of Patrasche was this. Into these great, sad(슬픈, 애석한) piles of stones, that reared(뒤쪽의, 후방의) their melancholy(구슬픈, 울적한) majesty(장엄함, 위풍당당함) above the crowded(붐비는, 복잡한; 빽빽한) roofs, the child Nello would many and many a time enter, and disappear((눈앞에서) 사라지다, 보이지 않게 되다) through their dark arched portals((건물의 웅장한) 정문[입구]), whilst Patrasche, left without upon the

35

pavement, would wearily and vainly ponder on
인도, 보도 / 지쳐서; 싫증이 나서 / 허사로, 헛되이 곰곰이 생각하다

what could be the charm which thus allured
매력(적인 요소) / 유혹하다, 꾀다

from him his inseparable and beloved compan-
갈라[떼어]놓을 수 없는 / (대단히) 사랑하는 친구, 벗

ion.

Once or twice he did essay to see for himself,
시도하다, 기도하다

clattering up the steps with his milk-cart behind
달그락[털커덕]거리며 가다[움직이다] / 우유 수레

him; but thereon he had been always sent back
그것에 대해 / 늘, 언제나 / 돌려 보내다

again summarily by a tall custodian in black
즉석에서 / 관리인

clothes and silver chains of office; and fearful of
옷, 의복 / 은색 / 걱정[염려]하는

bringing his little master into trouble, he desist-
곤경에 처하다, 문제가 되다 / 그만두다

ed, and remained couched patiently before the
남아 있다 / 끈기 있게, 참을성 있게

churches until such time as the boy reappeared.
성당, 교회 / ~까지 / 다시 나타나다

It was not the fact of his going into them
(…라는) 점[실상/실제]; 사실

which disturbed Patrasche: he knew that people
불안하게 만들다 / 알다 / 사람

went to church: all the village went to the small,
모든; 전부, 다 / 작은, 적은

tumbledown, gray pile opposite the red wind-
금방이라도 무너질 듯한, 다 허물어져 가는 / … 맞은편의

mill.

What troubled him was that little Nello
걱정하다, 골치 아프게 생각하다

always looked strangely when he came out, al-
이상하게, 낯설게, 기이하게

ways very flushed or very pale; and whenever
빨간, 상기된 / 창백한, 핼쑥한

he returned home after such visitations would
돌아가다[오다] / 방문, 찾아감

36

sit silent and dreaming, not caring to play, but
말을 안 하는, 침묵을 지키는, 조용한

gazing out at the evening skies beyond the line
(가만히) 응시하다[바라보다   저녁   …저편에, …너머

of the canal, very subdued and almost sad.
운하   (기분이) 가라앉은, 까라진, 좀 우울한   슬픈, 애석한

What was it? wondered Patrasche. He
궁금하다, 궁금해하다

thought it could not be good or natural for the
생각하다   자연스러운, 정상적인, 당연한

little lad to be so grave, and in his dumb fashion
사내아이   심각한, 심상치 않은   벙어리의,; 말을 못[안] 하는

he tried all he could to keep Nello by him in the
시도하다

sunny fields or in the busy market-place.
화창한, 햇살 가득한   바쁜, 분주한   시장, 장터

But to the churches Nello would go: most
성당, 교회   가장

often of all would he go to the great cathedral;
자주, 흔히   대성당

and Patrasche, left without on the stones by the

iron fragments of Quentin Matsys's gate, would
철, 쇠   조각, 파편; 부스러기   캥탱 마시가 만든 대문

stretch himself and yawn and sigh, and even
기지개를 켜다; 죽 늘이다   하품하다   한숨쉬다

howl now and then, all in vain, until the doors
(길게) 울다[울부짖다]   헛된, 소용없는

closed and the child perforce came forth again,
필요해서, 부득이(=necessarily)

and winding his arms about the dog's neck
두르다, 감다   팔   목

would kiss him on his broad, tawney-colored
넓은   황갈색의

forehead, and murmur always the same words:
이마   중얼거리다   늘, 언제나   같은   말, 단어

"If I could only see them, Patrasche!--if I could
단지, 그저

only see them!"

What were they? pondered Patrasche, look-
숙고하다, 곰곰이 생각하다(=consider)
ing up with large, wistful, sympathetic eyes.
아쉬워하는   동정적인, 동정어린
One day, when the custodian was out of the
관리인
way and the doors left ajar, he got in for a mo-
약간 열린   잠깐, 잠시 동안
ment after his little friend and saw.

"They" were two great covered pictures on
커다란   (덮개로) 덮인, 씌운, 가린   그림
either side of the choir.
(두 개) 각각[양쪽](의)   합창단, 성가대; (교회의) 성가대석
Nello was kneeling, rapt as in an ecstasy,
무릎을 꿇은   완전히 몰입한, 넋이 빠진   황홀감, 황홀경
before the altar-picture of the Assumption, and
제단 그림   성모 마리아의 승천
when he noticed Patrasche, and rose and drew
주목하다, 알아차리다   일어나다   끌다
the dog gently out into the air, his face was wet
부드럽게   얼굴   젖다
with tears, and he looked up at the veiled places
눈물   베일로 가려진
as he passed them, and murmured to his comp
지나가다   중얼거리다   친구, 벗, 동행
anion.

"It is so terrible not to see them, Patra-
심한, 지독한
sche, just because one is poor and cannot pay!
가난한   지불하다
He never meant that the poor should not see
뜻하다, 의미하다   가난한 사람
them when he painted them, I am sure. He
(그림을) 그리다   확신하다
would have had us see them any day, every day:

that I am sure. And they keep them shrouded
뒤덮다, 가리다
there--shrouded in the dark, the beautiful
뒤덮다, 가리다   어둠   아름다운

38

things!--and they never feel the light, and no eyes look on them, unless rich people come and pay. If I could only see them, I would be content to die."

But he could not see them, and Patrasche could not help him, for to gain the silver piece that the church exacts as the price for looking on the glories of the Elevation of the Cross and the Descent of the Cross was a thing as utterly beyond the powers of either of them as it would have been to scale the heights of the cathedral spire.

They had never so much as a sou to spare: if they cleared enough to get a little wood for the stove, a little broth for the pot, it was the utmost they could do.

And yet the heart of the child was set in sore and endless longing upon beholding the greatness of the two veiled Rubens. The whole soul of the little Ardennois thrilled and stirred with an absorbing passion for Art.

Going on his ways through the old city in the
…을 지나[뚫고], … 사이로   도시

early days before the sun or the people had ris-
이른, 조기의   ~전에   또는   사람들   일어나다

en, Nello, who looked only a little peasant-boy,
소작농[소농]

with a great dog drawing milk to sell from door
~와 함께, 더불어   끌다   팔다 집집마다 다니며

to door, was in a heaven of dreams whereof Ru-
천국   무엇[어떤 것]에 대해

bens was the god.
신

Nello, cold and hungry, with stockingless
추운, 차가운   배고픈, 굶주린   양말을 신지 않은

feet in wooden shoes, and the winter winds
나막신   겨울 바람

blowing among his curls and lifting his poor
불다   ~사이로   곱슬곱슬한 머리카락 들다, 들어올리다

thin garments, was in a rapture of meditation,
얇은   옷, 의류   황홀감(=delight)   명상, 묵상

wherein all that he saw was the beautiful fair
어디에(서)

face of the Mary of the Assumption, with the
성모승천(루벤스의 명작 중 하나)

waves of her golden hair lying upon her shoul-
물결   황금색의   머리(카락)   어깨

ders, and the light of an eternal sun shining
빛   영원한   빛나다, 반짝이다

down upon her brow.
이마(=forehead)

Nello, reared in poverty, and buffeted by for-
기르다   가난, 빈곤   뒤흔들다   운명, 운

tune, and untaught in letters, and unheeded by
배우지 않은, 교육을 받지 않은   무시된, 관심을 받지 못한

men, had the compensation or the curse which
(좋지 않은 점을 완화해 주는) 보상[이득]   저주

is called Genius.
천재, 귀재; 특별한 재능

No one knew it. He as little as any. No one

knew it. Only indeed Patrasche, who, being
정말로, 실제로

with him always, saw him draw with chalk
upon the stones any and every thing that grew
or breathed, heard him on his little bed of hay
murmur all manner of timid, pathetic prayers to
the spirit of the great Master; watched his gaze
darken and his face radiate at the evening glow
of sunset or the rosy rising of the dawn; and felt
many and many a time the tears of a strange,
nameless pain and joy, mingled together, fall
hotly from the bright young eyes upon his own
wrinkled yellow forehead.

"I should go to my grave quite content if I
thought, Nello, that when thou growest a man
thou couldst own this hut and the little plot of
ground, and labor for thyself, and be called Baas
by thy neighbors," said the old man Jehan many
an hour from his bed.

For to own a bit of soil, and to be called
Baas--master--by the hamlet round, is to have
achieved the highest ideal of a Flemish peasant;
and the old soldier, who had wandered over all

the earth in his youth, and had brought nothing
back, deemed in his old age that to live and die
on one spot in contented humility was the fairest fate he could desire for his darling. But Nello
said nothing.

The same leaven was working in him that in
other times begat Rubens and Jordaens and the
Van Eycks, and all their wondrous tribe, and in
times more recent begat in the green country of
the Ardennes, where the Meuse washes thc old
walls of Dijon, the great artist of the Patroclus,
whose genius is too near us for us aright to mea-
sure its divinity.
Nello dreamed of other things in the future
than of tilling the little rood of earth, and living
under the wattle roof, and being called Baas by
neighbors a little poorer or a little less poor than
himself. The cathedral spire, where it rose beyond the fields in the ruddy evening skies or in
the dim, gray, misty mornings, said other things
to him than this.

But these he told only to Patrasche, whispering, childlike, his fancies in the dog's ear when they went together at their work through the fogs of the daybreak, or lay together at their rest among the rustling rushes by the water's side. For such dreams are not easily shaped into speech to awake the slow sympathies of human auditors; and they would only have sorely perplexed and troubled the poor old man bedridden in his corner, who, for his part, whenever he had trodden the streets of Antwerp, had thought the daub of blue and red that they called a Madonna, on the walls of the wine-shop where he drank his sou's worth of black beer, quite as good as any of the famous altar-pieces for which the stranger folk travelled far and wide into Flanders from every land on which the good sun shone.

There was only one other beside Patrasche to whom Nello could talk at all of his daring fantasies. This other was little Alois, who lived

at the old red mill on the grassy mound, and
방앗간, 제분소 　 풀로 덮인 　 흙[돌]더미, 언덕

whose father, the miller, was the best-to-do hus-
아버지 　 방앗간 주인, 제분업자 　 농부, (농업) 전문가

bandman in all the village.
(시골) 마을, 부락, 촌락

Little Alois was only a pretty baby with soft
예쁜, 귀여운 　 부드러운

round, rosy features, made lovely by those sweet
동그란 　 장밋빛, 붉은 특징, 이목구비(의 각 부분) 　 달콤한

dark eyes that the Spanish rule has left in so
짙은, 어두운 　 스페인의 　 통치 　 남다

many a Flemish face, in testimony of the Alvan
플랜더스 사람의 　 증거, 증언

dominion, as Spanish art has left broadsown
지배[통치](권) 　 스페인 미술[예술]

throughout the country majestic palaces and
도처에, 두루, 전체에 걸쳐 　 장엄한, 위풍당당한 궁전

stately courts, gilded house-fronts and sculp-
위풍당당한, 위엄 있는 　 금박을 입힌, 도금을 한 　 조각된, 소각품의

tured lintels--histories in blazonry and poems in
상인방(문틀·창틀의 일부로 문·창문을 가로지르게 되어 있는 가로대)

stone.

Little Alois was often with Nello and Patra-
자주, 흔히

sche. They played in the fields, they ran in the
놀다, (게임놀이 등을) 하다 　 달리다(run)

snow, they gathered the daisies and bilberries,
눈 　 (여기 저기 있는 것을) 모으다[챙기다] 　 월귤나무 (열매)

they went up to the old gray church together,
회색, 잿빛 교회, 성당

and they often sat together by the broad wood-
앉다(sit) 　 폭 넓은 모닥불

fire in the mill-house.
방앗간 집

Little Alois, indeed, was the richest child in
정말, 참으로 　 가장 부유한(rich의 최상급)

the hamlet. She had neither brother nor sister;
작은 시골 마을 　 neither A nor B : A도 아니고 B도 아니다

her blue serge dress had never a hole in it; at
서지(짜임이 튼튼한 모직물) 　 구멍

44

Kermesse she had as many gilded nuts and Agni
Dei in sugar as her hands could hold; and when
she went up for her first communion her flaxen
curls were covered with a cap of richest Mechlin lace, which had been her mother's and her
grandmother's before it came to her.

Men spoke already, though she had but
twelve years, of the good wife she would be for
their sons to woo and win; but she herself was
a little gay, simple child, in nowise conscious of
her heritage, and she loved no playfellows so
well as Jehan Daas's grandson and his dog.

One day her father, Baas Cogez, a good man,
어느 날 아버지 나리; 이름 앞에 붙이는 경칭

but somewhat stern, came on a pretty group
어느 정도, 약간 엄격한, 단호한; 가혹한, 용서 없는 무리, 집단, 그룹

in the long meadow behind the mill, where the
(특히 건초를 만들기 위한) 목초지

aftermath had that day been cut.
후유증, 여파, 뒷일 베다, 자르다

It was his little daughter sitting amidst the
딸 ~속에[사이에]

hay, with the great tawny head of Patrasche
건초 큰, 거대한 황갈색의 머리

on her lap, and many wreaths of poppies and
무릎 화환, 꽃목걸이 양귀비

blue corn-flowers round them both: on a clean
수레국화(청색 꽃이 피는 야생화의 일종)

smooth slab of pine wood the boy Nello drew
매끈한, 매끄러운 평판, 판 그리다

their likeness with a stick of charcoal.
초상화, (어떤 사람과 아주 닮은) 화상 숯, 목탄

The miller stood and looked at the portrait
방앗간[제분소] 주인[일꾼] ~을 (자세히) 살피다 초상화

with tears in his eyes, it was so strangely like,
눈물 이상하게, 기이하게

and he loved his only child closely and well.
외동(딸·아들)

Then he roughly chid the little girl for idling
거칠게, 험하게 게으름, 나태함

there whilst her mother needed her within, and
=WHILE (…을) 필요로 하다 ~안으로[에서]

sent her indoors crying and afraid: then, turn-
보내다 실내의, 집안의

ing, he snatched the wood from Nello's hands.
와락 붙잡다, 잡아채다, 잡아뺐다,

"Dost do much of such folly?" he asked, but
바보짓, 어리석음, 어리석은 행동

there was a tremble in his voice.
떨림, 전율

Nello colored and hung his head.
(당황하여 얼굴이) 붉어지다

"I draw everything I see," he murmured.
중얼거리나

47

The miller was silent: then he stretched his
말을 안 하는, 침묵을 지키는, 조용한
hand out with a franc in it.
프랑(스위스 등의 화폐 단위)

"It is folly, as I say, and evil waste of time:
낭비하다, 헛되이 쓰다
nevertheless, it is like Alois, and will please the
그렇기는 하지만, 그럼에도 불구하고   (남을) 기쁘게 하다
house-mother. Take this silver bit for it and
갖다, 취하다   은화
leave it for me."
두다, 남기다

The color died out of the face of the young
사라지다, 멸종되다   얼굴   젊은, 어린
Ardennois; he lifted his head and put his hands
아르덴 사람   들다, 들어올리다
behind his back.
~뒤로   등

"Keep your money and the portrait both,
유지하다, 지키다   돈   초상화   놀 나
Baas Cogez," he said, simply. "You have been
그냥 (간단히), 그저 (단순히)
often good to me."
자주, 흔히, 보통

Then he called Patrasche to him, and walked
부르다   걸어가다
away across the field.
~을 가로질러

"I could have seen them with that franc," he
murmured to Patrasche, "but I could not sell her
중얼거리다   팔다
picture--not even for them."
그림   ~라 해도, 조차

Baas Cogez went into his mill-house sore
~안으로 들어가다   화가 난, 감정이 상한
troubled in his mind.
걱정하는, 불안해하는

"That lad must not be so much with Alois,"
he said to his wife that night. "Trouble may
come of it hereafter: he is fifteen now, and she is
twelve; and the boy is comely of face and form."

"And he is a good lad and a loyal," said the
housewife, feasting her eyes on the piece of pine
wood where it was throned above the chimney
with a cuckoo clock in oak and a Calvary in wax.

"Yea, I do not gainsay that," said the miller,
draining his pewter flagon.

"Then, if what you think of were ever to
come to pass," said the wife, hesitatingly, "would
it matter so much? She will have enough for
both, and one cannot be better than happy."

"You are a woman, and therefore a fool,"
said the miller, harshly, striking his pipe on the
table. "The lad is naught but a beggar, and, with
these painter's fancies, worse than a beggar.
Have a care that they are not together in the future, or I will send the child to the surer keeping
of the nuns of the Sacred Heart."

The poor mother was terrified, and promised
(몹시) 무서워하다, 겁에 질리다　약속하다
humbly to do his will. Not that she could bring
겸손하여, 황송하여　　의지
herself altogether to separate the child from her
완전히, 전적으로　분리하다, 나누다; 떨어지게 하다
favorite playmate, nor did the miller even desire
매우 좋아하는, 총애하는　바라다, 원하다
that extreme of cruelty to a young lad who was
극도의, 극심한, 지나친　잔인하게, 모질게
guilty of nothing except poverty.
유죄의, (잘못된 일에 대해) 책임이 있는　가난, 빈곤

But there were many ways in which little
방법, 방식
Alois was kept away from her chosen compan-
~에게서 멀리 떼어내다　선택한, 좋아하는(choose)
ion; and Nello, being a boy proud and quiet and
자존심[자부심]이 강한
sensitive, was quickly wounded, and ceased to
세심한, 예민한, 민감한　상처를 입다　중단되다, 그치다
turn his own steps and those of Patrasche, as
he had been used to do with every moment of
~하곤 하다　순간
leisure, to the old red mill upon the slope.
여가, 한가　(산)비탈, 경사면, 언덕

What his offence was he did not know: he
위법[범법] 행위, 범죄
supposed he had in some manner angered
(…일 것이라고) 생각하다, 추정[추측]하다　화나게 하다
Baas Cogez by taking the portrait of Alois in the
초상화
meadow; and when the child who loved him
목초지, 초원
would run to him and nestle her hand in his,
따뜻이 앉다[눕다]
he would smile at her very sadly and say with a
미소 짓다　슬프게
tender concern for her before himself.
우려, 걱정, 근심

"Nay, Alois, do not anger your father. He
(아니) (화나게 하다) (아버지)
thinks that I make you idle, dear, and he is not
(생각하다) (게으른, 나태한)
pleased that you should be with me. He is a
(기쁘게 하다, 즐겁게 하다)
good man and loves you well: we will not anger
(좋은, 착한)
him, Alois."

But it was with a sad heart that he said it,
(슬픈) (마음, 심장, 가슴)
and the earth did not look so bright to him as
(밝은, 눈부신, 빛나는)
it had used to do when he went out at sunrise
(~하곤 하다) (동틀녘, 일출)
under the poplars down the straight roads with
(~아래, ~밑에) ((굽거나 휘지 않고) 곧은, 똑바른)
Patrasche.

The old red mill had been a landmark to
(랜드마크, 표지)
him, and he had been used to pause by it, going
(잠시 멈추다)
and coming, for a cheery greeting with its people
(쾌활한, 명랑한)
as her little flaxen head rose above the low mill-
(아마 빛의, 금발의 (=blonde)) (방앗간의 쪽문)
wicket, and her little rosy hands had held out a
(발그레한, 장밋빛의)
bone or a crust to Patrasche.
(뼈) (빵껍질)
Now the dog looked wistfully at a closed
(아쉬운 듯이, 생각에 잠겨)
door, and the boy went on without pausing, with
(멈추지 않고)
a pang at his heart, and the child sat within with
(갑자기 격렬하게 일어나는 육체적·정신적 고통·아픔)
tears dropping slowly on the knitting to which
she was set on her little stool by the stove; and
((등받이와 팔걸이가 없는) 의자, 스툴)

Baas Cogez, working among his sacks and his
mill-gear, would harden his will and say to himself.

"It is best so. The lad is all but a beggar, and
full of idle, dreaming fooleries. Who knows what
mischief might not come of it in the future?"
So he was wise in his generation, and would
not have the door unbarred, except upon rare
and formal occasion, which seemed to have
neither warmth nor mirth in them to the two
children, who had been accustomed so long to
a daily gleeful, careless, happy interchange of
greeting, speech, and pastime, with no other
watcher of their sports or auditor of their fancies
than Patrasche, sagely shaking the brazen bells
of his collar and responding with all a dog's
swift sympathies to their every change of mood.
All this while the little panel of pine wood
remained over the chimney in the mill-kitchen
with the cuckoo clock and the waxen Calvary,
and sometimes it seemed to Nello a little hard

that whilst his gift was accepted he himself
선물 (기꺼이) 받아들이다, 인정하다
should be denied.
사실이 아니라고 말하다, 부인[부정]하다
But he did not complain: it was his habit to
불평하다, 항의하다 버릇, 습관
be quiet: old Jehan Daas had said ever to him.
조용한, 고요한 언제나, 항상
"We are poor: we must take what God sends-
가난한 ~해야 하다 보내주다
-the ill with the good: the poor cannot choose."
문제, 해악; 병; 불운 고르다, 선택하다
To which the boy had always listened in
늘 경청하다; 귀 기울여 듣다
silence, being reverent of his old grandfather;
침묵, 고요 숭배하는(=respectful) 할아버지
but nevertheless a certain vague, sweet hope,
그렇기는 하지만, 그럼에도 불구하고 희미한, 어렴풋한 희망, 소망
such as beguiles the children of genius, had
(마음을) 끌다, 이끌다 천재(성), 귀재
whispered in his heart.
속삭이다

"Yet the poor do choose sometimes--choose
빈자, 가난한 사람 고르다, 선택하다
to be great, so that men cannot say them nay."
위대한, 커다란 말하다 아니다(no)
And he thought so still in his innocence.
아직(도) (계속해서)결백, 무죄; 천진

And one day, when the little Alois, finding
발견하다, 보다
him by chance alone among the cornfields by
우연히 혼자, 외로이 옥수수밭
the canal, ran to him and held him close, and
운하 달려오다 붙잡다
sobbed piteously because the morrow would be
흐느껴 울다 애처롭게, 가엾게 그 다음 날, 내일
her saint's day, and for the first time in all her
영명축일 첫 번째, 처음의
life her parents had failed to bid him to the little
부모 …하지 않다 (…에) 초대하다 (to)

supper and romp in the great barns with which her feast-day was always celebrated, Nello had kissed her and murmured to her in firm faith.

"It shall be different one day, Alois. One day that little bit of pine wood that your father has of mine shall be worth its weight in silver; and he will not shut the door against me then. Only love me always, dear little Alois, only love me always, and I will be great."

"And if I do not love you?" the pretty child asked, pouting a little through her tears, and moved by the instinctive coquetries of her sex.

Nello's eyes left her face and wandered to the distance, where in the red and gold of the Flemish night the cathedral spire rose.

There was a smile on his face so sweet and yet so sad that little Alois was awed by it.

"I will be great still," he said under his breath--"great still, or die, Alois."

"You do not love me," said the little spoilt child, pushing him away.

But the boy shook his head and smiled, and
went on his way through the tall yellow corn,
seeing as in a vision some day in a fair future
when he should come into that old familiar land
and ask Alois of her people, and be not refused
or denied, but received in honor, whilst the
village folk should throng to look upon him and
say in one another's ears.

"Dost see him? He is a king among men,
for he is a great artist and the world speaks his
name; and yet he was only our poor little Nello,
who was a beggar as one may say, and only got
his bread by the help of his dog."

And he thought how he would fold his
grandsire in furs and purples, and portray him
as the old man is portrayed in the Family in the
chapel of St. Jacques; and of how he would hang
the throat of Patrasche with a collar of gold,
and place him on his right hand, and say to the
people, "This was once my only friend."

And of how he would build himself a great

white marble palace, and make to himself luxuriant gardens of pleasure, on the slope looking outward to where the cathedral spire rose, and not dwell in it himself, but summon to it, as to a home, all men young and poor and friendless, but of the will to do mighty things; and of how he would say to them always, if they sought to bless his name.

"Nay, do not thank me--thank Rubens. Without him, what should I have been?"

And these dreams, beautiful, impossible, innocent, free of all selfishness, full of heroical worship, were so closely about him as he went that he was happy--happy even on this sad anniversary of Alois's saint's day.

When he and Patrasche went home by themselves to the little dark hut and the meal of black bread, whilst in the mill-house all the children of the village sang and laughed, and ate the big round cakes of Dijon and the almond gingerbread of Brabant, and danced in the great barn

to the light of the stars and the music of flute
별   음악   플루트
and fiddle.
바이올린(=violin)

"Never mind, Patrasche," he said, with his
괜찮다, 신경 쓰지 마라, 됐다

arms round the dog's neck as they both sat in
팔   두르다   목   둘 다, 양쪽 모두

the door of the hut, where the sounds of the
오두막   소리

mirth at the mill came down to them on the
웃음소리, 즐거움

night air--"never mind. It shall all be changed
공기   바꾸다, 변하다

by and by."
머지않아, 곧; 점점

He believed in the future: Patrasche, of more
믿다, 신뢰하다   미래, 장래   더 많은

experience and of more philosophy, thought
경험   철학

that the loss of the mill supper in the present
분실, 상실, 손실   저녁식사   현재, 지금

was ill compensated by dreams of milk and
보상하다(=make up for)   우유

honey in some vague hereafter. And Patrasche
꿀   모호한, 애매한   이후로, 장차

growled whenever he passed by Baas Cogez.
으르렁거리다   지나가다

"This is Alois's name-day, is it not?" said the
영명일

old man Daas that night from the corner where
밤   구석

he was stretched upon his bed of sacking.
늘이다, 기지개를 켜다   부대 만드는 천(=sackcloth)

The boy gave a gesture of assent: he wished
몸짓, 제스처   찬성하다, 동의하다 바라다, 원하다

that the old man's memory had erred a little,
기억(력)   실수를 범하다, 잘못하다

instead of keeping such sure account.
~대신에   분명한, 확실한

"And why not there?" his grandfather pursued. "Thou hast never missed a year before, Nello."

"Thou art too sick to leave," murmured the lad, bending his handsome head over the bed.

"Tut! tut! Mother Nulette would have come and sat with me, as she does scores of times. What is the cause, Nello?" the old man persisted. "Thou surely hast not had ill words with the little one?"

"Nay, grandfather--never," said the boy quickly, with a hot color in his bent face. "Simply and truly, Baas Cogez did not have me asked this year. He has taken some whim against me."

"But thou hast done nothing wrong?"

"That I know--nothing. I took the portrait of Alois on a piece of pine: that is all."

"Ah!" The old man was silent: the truth suggested itself to him with the boy's innocent answer.

He was tied to a bed of dried leaves in the
묶다, 매다   마른, 말린 잎사귀
corner of a wattle hut, but he had not wholly
구석   윗가지   완전히, 전적으로
forgotten what the ways of the world were like.
잊다, 잊어버리다   방식

He drew Nello's fair head fondly to his breast
끌어당기다   금발의   애정을 듬뿍 담고   가슴
with a tenderer gesture.
        더 부드러운

"Thou art very poor, my child," he said with
                가난한
a quiver the more in his aged, trembling voice--
   (가볍게) 떨다[떨리다](=tremble)   떨리는, 흔들리는
"so poor! It is very hard for thee."
                        엄한, 힘든, 가혹한

"Nay, I am rich," murmured Nello; and
        부유한   중얼거리다
in his innocence he thought so--rich with the
      전진함, 순진함
imperishable powers that are mightier than the
불멸의, 불후의 (=enduring)   더 힘센, 더 강력한
might of kings.
   힘

And he went and stood by the door of the
        가다(go)   stand   ~옆에
hut in the quiet autumn night, and watched the
        조용한, 고요한 가을   지켜보다
stars troop by and the tall poplars bend and
별   부대, 무리   키 큰 포플러 나무
shiver in the wind. All the casements of the mill-
(가볍게) (몸을) 떨다; 흔들리다   여닫이창
house were lighted, and every now and then the
            불을 켜다[밝히다]   때때로, 가끔
notes of the flute came to him.

The tears fell down his cheeks, for he was
눈물   떨어지다   뺨, 볼   왜냐하면, ~때문에
but a child, yet he smiled, for he said to himself,
      하지만, 그래도
"In the future!"
      장래, 미래

He stayed there until all was quite still and dark, then he and Patrasche went within and slept together, long and deeply, side by side.

Now he had a secret which only Patrasche knew. There was a little out-house to the hut, which no one entered but himself--a dreary place, but with abundant clear light from the north.

Here he had fashioned himself rudely an easel in rough lumber, and here on a great gray sea of stretched paper he had given shape to one of the innumerable fancies which possessed his brain.

No one had ever taught him anything; colors he had no means to buy; he had gone without bread many a time to procure even the few rude vehicles that he had here; and it was only in black or white that he could fashion the things he saw. This great figure which he had drawn here in chalk was only an old man sitting on a fallen tree--only that. He had seen old Michel the woodman sitting so at evening many a time.

He had never had a soul to tell him of outline

or perspective, of anatomy or of shadow, and

yet he had given all the weary, worn-out age, all

the sad, quiet patience, all the rugged, careworn

pathos of his original, and given them so that

the old lonely figure was a poem, sitting there,

meditative and alone, on the dead tree, with the

darkness of the descending night behind him.

It was rude, of course, in a way, and had

many faults, no doubt; and yet it was real, true

in nature, true in art, and very mournful, and in

a manner beautiful.

Patrasche had lain quiet countless hours

watching its gradual creation after the labor of

each day was done, and he knew that Nello had

a hope--vain and wild perhaps, but strongly

cherished--of sending this great drawing to

compete for a prize of two hundred francs a year

which it was announced in Antwerp would be

open to every lad of talent, scholar or peasant,

under eighteen, who would attempt to win it

18세 (힘든 일을) 시도하다, 애써 해보다

with some unaided work of chalk or pencil.

도움을 받지 않는 연필

Three of the foremost artists in the town of

가장 중요한[유명한], 맨 앞에 위치한

Rubens were to be the judges and elect the vic-

심사하다 뽑다, 선출하다

tor according to his merits.

…에 따라서 가치 있는[훌륭한] 요소, 장점

All the spring and summer and autumn

봄 여름 가을

Nello had been at work upon this treasure,

~에 애쓰다[공들이다] 보물

which, if triumphant, would build him his first

크게 성공한, 큰 승리를 거눈 첫 걸음

step toward independence and the mysteries

~쪽으로 독립, 자립 신비, 불가사의

of the art which he blindly, ignorantly, and yet

맹목적으로, 무턱대고 무식[무지]하게

passionately adored. He said nothing to any one:

열렬히, 격렬하게 흠모하다, 사모하다, 동경하다

his grandfather would not have understood, and

할아버지 이해하다, 알다

little Alois was lost to him. Only to Patrasche he

되찾을 수 없는, 놓쳐 버린

told all, and whispered.

알리다, 전하다, 말하다 속삭이다

"Rubens would give it me, I think, if he

주다 생각하다

knew."

알다(know의 과거)

Patrasche thought so too, for he knew that

생각하다(think) 역시, 또한

Rubens had loved dogs or he had never painted

그림을 그리다

them with such exquisite fidelity; and men who

매우 아름다운, 정교한 충실함

loved dogs were, as Patrasche knew, always

늘, 언제나

pitiful.

측은한, 가련한

The drawings were to go in on the first day
그림   첫째
of December, and the decision be given on the
12월   결정, 판단
twenty-fourth, so that he who should win might
24   이기다
rejoice with all his people at the Christmas
크게[대단히] 기뻐하다
season.
(1년 중에서 특정한 활동이 행해지는) 철[시즌]
    In the twilight of a bitter wintry day, and
          황혼, 땅거미   격렬한, 혹독한 겨울다운, 혹한의
with a beating heart, now quick with hope, now
        두근대는, 쿵쿵 뛰는   희망을 품고
faint with fear, Nello placed the great picture on
희미한, 약한   공포, 두려움 놓다, 두다   그림
his little green milk-cart, and took it, with the

help of Patrasche, into the town, and there left
도움, 지원   도시   남겨두다
it, as enjoined, at the doors of a public building.
        (무엇을 하도록) 명하다[이르다]   대중을 위한, 공공의
    "Perhaps it is worth nothing at all. How can
      아마, 어쩌면   가치 있는   전혀
I tell?" he thought, with the heart-sickness of a
                                슬픔에 잠김, 상심함
great timidity.
      겁 많음, 수줍음, 소심함, 자신 없음
    Now that he had left it there, it seemed to
              남겨두다
him so hazardous, so vain, so foolish, to dream
        위험한   헛된   바보같은, 멍청한 꿈을 꾸다
that he, a little lad with bare feet, who barely
              사내아이   헐벗은, 벌거벗은   간신히, 가까스로
knew his letters, could do anything at which
        글자, 문자   무엇, 아무것
great painters, real artists, could ever deign to
    화가   진정한 예술가   ~한다는 듯이 굴다
look.

    Yet he took heart as he went by the cathe-
        힘내다, 자신감을 얻다 ~옆을 지나가다   대성당

63

dral: the lordly form of Rubens seemed to rise
위풍당당한, 훌륭한

from the fog and the darkness, and to loom in
안개 어둠 불쑥 나타나다

its magnificence before him, whilst the lips, with
장려(壯麗), 웅장, 장엄, 기품, 훌륭함　(=while)　입술

their kindly smile, seemed to him to murmur.
친절한　중얼거리다

"Nay, have courage! It was not by a weak
아니　용기, 힘, 담력　약한, 힘 없는

heart and by faint fears that I wrote my name
미약한, 열의 없는　쓰다, 알리다　이름

for all time upon Antwerp."
역대의

Nello ran home through the cold night,
·을 뚫고, ~을 지나　추운, 차가운

comforted. He had done his best: the rest must
위로를 받은, 안락해진　최선을 다하다　나머지

be as God willed, he thought, in that innocent,
뜻, 의지　순수한, 무고한

unquestioning faith which had been taught him
의문 없는, 의심하지 않는　믿음, 신념

in the little gray chapel among the willows and
(교회·대성당 등의) 소예배당, 분회당

the poplar-trees.

The winter was very sharp already. That
겨울　날카로운; 선명한, 뚜렷한, 분명한

night, after they reached the hut, snow fell; and
~뒤에　닿다, 도착하다　눈　내리다, 떨어지다

fell for very many days after that, so that the
많은

paths and the divisions in the fields were all
(작은) 길　경계선　들판

obliterated, and all the smaller streams were
(흔적을) 없애다[지우다]　더 작은　시내, 개천

frozen over, and the cold was intense upon the
얼다, 얼어붙다　추위　극심한, 강렬한(=extreme)

plains.
평원

Then, indeed, it became hard work to go
정말로, 실제로　힘든, 고된, 어려운

round for the milk while the world was all dark,
세상, 세계 어두운
and carry it through the darkness to the silent
나르다, 운반하다 ~을 뚫고[통과하여] 어둠 조용한, 고요한
town.

Hard work, especially for Patrasche, for the
유난히, 특별히
passage of the years, that were only bringing
(시간의) 흐름[경과] 가져오다, 가져다주다
Nello a stronger youth, were bringing him old
더 힘센[강한] 젊음
age, and his joints were stiff and his bones ached
나이 관절 뻣뻣한 뼈 아프다
often.
자주, 흔히
But he would never give up his share of the
포기하다, 그만두다 몫, 지분
labor. Nello would fain have spared him and
노동, 근로 기꺼이, 흔쾌히 피하게[면하게] 해 주다
drawn the cart himself, but Patrasche would not
끌다
allow it.
허락하다, 용납하다
All he would ever permit or accept was the
허용[허락]하다 받아들이다
help of a thrust from behind to the truck as it
도움 추진력 ~뒤에서
lumbered along through the ice-ruts.
느릿느릿 움직이다 얼어붙은 바퀴 자국
Patrasche had lived in harness, and he was
마구(馬具), 벨트
proud of it. He suffered a great deal sometimes
자랑스러워하다, 자랑으로 여기다 시달리다, 고통받다
from frost, and the terrible roads, and the
서리 끔찍한, 심한, 지독한
rheumatic pains of his limbs, but he only drew
류머티즘의; 류머티즘에 걸린 팔, 다리
his breath hard and bent his stout neck, and
숨, 호흡 튼튼한, 굳센
trod onward with steady patience.
밟다, 디디다(tread)

"Rest thee at home, Patrasche--it is time thou didst rest--and I can quite well push in the cart by myself," urged Nello many a morning; but Patrasche, who understood him aright, would no more have consented to stay at home than a veteran soldier to shirk when the charge was sounding; and every day he would rise and place himself in his shafts, and plod along over the snow through the fields that his four round feet had left their print upon so many, many years.

"One must never rest till one dies," thought Patrasche; and sometimes it seemed to him that that time of rest for him was not very far off. His sight was less clear than it had been, and it gave him pain to rise after the night's sleep, though he would never lie a moment in his straw when once the bell of the chapel tolling five let him know that the daybreak of labor had begun.

"My poor Patrasche, we shall soon lie quiet together, you and I," said old Jehan Daas, stretching out to stroke the head of Patrasche with the old withered hand which had always shared with him its one poor crust of bread; and the hearts of the old man and the old dog ached together with one thought: When they were gone, who would care for their darling?

One afternoon, as they came back from Antwerp over the snow, which had become hard and smooth as marble over all the Flemish plains, they found dropped in the road a pretty little puppet, a tambourine--player, all scarlet and gold, about six inches high, and, unlike greater personages when Fortune lets them drop, quite unspoiled and unhurt by its fall.

It was a pretty toy. Nello tried to find its owner, and, failing, thought that it was just the thing to please Alois.

It was quite night when he passed the mill-house: he knew the little window of her room.

It could be no harm, he thought, if he gave her
his little piece of treasure-trove, they had been
playfellows so long.

해, 피해, 손해 / 주다 / (임자가 누군지 모르는) 보물 / 어릴 때 친구(=playmate)

There was a shed with a sloping roof beneath
her casement: he climbed it and tapped softly at
the lattice: there was a little light within.

(작은) 헛간 / 경사진(inclined), 비탈진(slanting), 비스듬한 / 여닫이창 / 기어 올라가다 / 톡톡 두드리다 / 격자, 격자 모양의 것 / 불빛

The child opened it and looked out half
frightened. Nello put the tambourine-player
into her hands.

열다 / 내다보다 / 겁먹은, 무서워하는 / 놓다, 두다

"Here is a doll I found in the snow, Alois.
Take it," he whispered--"take it, and God bless
thee, dear!"

인형 / 발견하다 / 눈 / 속삭이다 / …에게 축복이 있기를!

He slid down from the shed-roof before she
had time to thank him, and ran off through the
darkness.

미끄러지다, 미끄러지듯이(slide의 과거·과거분사) / ~전에 / 감사하다, 고마워하다 / 뛰어 달아나다 / 어둠

That night there was a fire at the mill.
Outbuildings and much corn were destroyed,
although the mill itself and the dwelling-house
were unharmed.

불, 화재 / 바깥채, 별채 / [집합적] 곡물, 곡식 / 파괴하다, 말살하다 / (비록) …이긴 하지만(=though) / 주거(지), 주택, 거주하는 본채 / 해를 입지 않은, 피해 없는

All the village was out in terror, and engines
came tearing through the snow from Antwerp.

모두, 전부 / 깜짝 놀라서 / 엔진, 소방차 / 맹렬히, 냅다, 미친 듯이

The miller was insured, and would lose
nothing: nevertheless, he was in furious wrath,
and declared aloud that the fire was due to no
accident, but to some foul intent.

Nello, awakened from his sleep, ran to help
with the rest: Baas Cogez thrust him angrily
aside.

"Thou wert loitering here after dark," he said
roughly. "I believe, on my soul, that thou dost
know more of the fire than any one."

Nello heard him in silence, stupefied, not
supposing that any one could say such things
except in jest, and not comprehending how any
one could pass a jest at such a time.

Nevertheless, the miller said the brutal thing
openly to many of his neighbors in the day that
followed; and though no serious charge was
ever preferred against the lad, it got bruited
about that Nello had been seen in the mill-yard

after dark on some unspoken errand, and that
he bore Baas Cogez a grudge for forbidding his

intercourse with little Alois; and so the hamlet, which followed the sayings of its richest land-owner servilely, and whose families all hoped to secure the riches of Alois in some future time for their sons, took the hint to give grave looks and cold words to old Jehan Daas's grandson.

No one said anything to him openly, but all the village agreed together to humor the miller's prejudice, and at the cottages and farms where Nello and Patrasche called every morning for the milk for Antwerp, downcast glances and brief phrases replaced to them the broad smiles and cheerful greetings to which they had been always used.

No one really credited the miller's absurd suspicion, nor the outrageous accusations born of them, but the people were all very poor and very ignorant, and the one rich man of the place had pronounced against him.

Nello, in his innocence and his friendless-ness, had no strength to stem the popular tide.

"Thou art very cruel to the lad," the miller's
잔혹한, 잔인한
wife dared to say, weeping, to her lord. "Sure
감히 …하다   울다, 눈물을 흘리다
he is an innocent lad and a faithful, and would
순수한, 순진한   충실한, 충직한, 신의 있는
never dream of any such wickedness, however
사악, 부정; 악의, 짓궂음
sore his heart might be."
아픈, 고통스러운

But Baas Cogez being an obstinate man, hav-
고집 센, 완강한(=stubborn)
ing once said a thing held to it doggedly, though
한 번   억세게, 완강하게
in his innermost soul he knew well the injustice
가장 사적인[내밀한]   불평등; 부당함
that he was committing.
(그릇된 일·범죄를) 저지르다[범하다]

Meanwhile, Nello endured the injury done
(다른 일이 일어나고 있는) 그 동안에 견디다, 참다, 인내하다   (마음의) 상처[피해]
against him with a certain proud patience that
자랑스러운 인내력, 인내심
disdained to complain: he only gave way a little
업신여기다, 무시하다   불평하다, 항의하다
when he was quite alone with old Patrasche.
혼자, 외로이

Besides, he thought, "If it should win! They
게다가, 뿐만 아니라   이기다, 우승하다
will be sorry then, perhaps."
아마, 어쩌면

Still, to a boy not quite sixteen, and who had
아직, 여전히   16
dwelt in one little world all his short life, and in
살다, 거주하다   작은, 조그만   짧은 인생, 삶
his childhood had been caressed and applauded
어린시절   애무하다, 어루만지다 박수치다, 갈채를 보내다
on all sides, it was a hard trial to have the whole
힘든   시험, 시련
of that little world turn against him for naught.
…에 반대하여[맞서]   제로 , 영, 무(無)

71

Especially hard in that bleak, snow-bound,
유난히, 특별히   암울한, 절망적인   눈에 갇힌
famine-stricken winter-time, when the only light
기아에 시달리는, 기근으로 고통받고 있는   오직, 단지
and warmth there could be found abode beside
따뜻함, 온기   거주지, 집 ~옆에서
the village hearths and in the kindly greetings of
난로 (바닥), 난로 부근[근처]   친절한, 다정한
neighbors.

In the winter-time all drew nearer to each
더 가까운   서로서로
other, all to all, except to Nello and Patrasche,
~를 제외하고, ~빼고
with whom none now would have anything to
do, and who were left to fare as they might with
the old paralyzed, bedridden man in the little
마비된, 반신불수의   아파서 누워 있는, 자리보전을 하고 있는
cabin, whose fire was often low, and whose
오두막집   불   자주, 흔히   낮은, 저조한
board was often without bread, for there was
판자, 널   ~없는   빵
a buyer from Antwerp who had taken to drive
바이어, (사업적인) 구매자
his mule in of a day for the milk of the various
노새   여러 가지의, 다양한
dairies, and there were only three or four of the
셋   또는 넷
people who had refused his terms of purchase
거절하다, 거부하다   (정해진) 기간   구입, 구매, 매입
and remained faithful to the little green cart.
계속[여전히] …이다, (없어지지 않고) 남다
So that the burden which Patrasche drew
부담, 짐   끌다
had become very light, and the centime-picces
가벼운   상팀(프랑스의 화폐 단위, 1/100 프랑)
in Nello's pouch had become, alas! very small
주머니, 작은 가방   세상에! 맙소사!
likewise.
똑같이, 비슷하게

The dog would stop, as usual, at all the familiar gates, which were now closed to him, and look up at them with wistful, mute appeal; and it cost the neighbors a pang to shut their doors and their hearts, and let Patrasche draw his cart on again, empty. Nevertheless, they did it, for they desired to please Baas Cogez.

Noel was close at hand.
크리스마스(의 계절).

The weather was very wild and cold. The
날씨, 기후   험한, 거친   추운
snow was six feet deep, and the ice was firm
피트(길이의 단위로 약 12인치 또는 30.48센티미터)   굳은, 단단한
enough to bear oxen and men upon it every-
황소
where.

At this season the little village was always
계절, 시즌   늘, 언제나
gay and cheerful. At the poorest dwelling there
즐거운   명랑한, 쾌활한   가장 가난한   거주자
were possets and cakes, joking and dancing,
우유술(과거 뜨거운 우유에 맥주나 와인을 섞어 마시던 술)
sugared saints and gilded Jesus.
설탕으로 만든 성자상   금박을 입힌 예수상
The merry Flemish bells jingled everywhere
즐거운, 유쾌한   (듣기 좋게) 딸랑[쌀랑/뎅그랑]거리다
on the horses; everywhere within doors some
말
well-filled soup-pot sang and smoked over the
가득 찬, 든든한   죽 솥, 수프 냄비   연기를 피우다
stove; and everywhere over the snow without
난로
laughing maidens pattered in bright kerchiefs
웃는   처녀, 아가씨   재잘거리다(chatter) (목이나 머리에 두르는) 스카프
and stout kirtles, going to and from the mass.
튼튼한   커틀(길고 낙낙한 가운)   미사
Only in the little hut it was very dark and very
오직   오두막   어두운
cold.
추운, 차가운
Nello and Patrasche were left utterly alone,
완전히, 전적으로
for one night in the week before the Christmas
주(週), 일주일
Day, Death entered there, and took away from
죽음   들어오다, 입장하다   가져가다, 데려가다
life forever old Jehan Daas, who had never
생명   영원히

known life aught save its poverty and its pains.
He had long been half dead, incapable of
any movement except a feeble gesture, and
powerless for anything beyond a gentle word;
and yet his loss fell on them both with a great
horror in it: they mourned him passionately.
He had passed away from them in his
sleep, and when in the gray dawn they learned
their bereavement, unutterable solitude and
desolation seemed to close around them.
He had long been only a poor, feeble,
paralyzed old man, who could not raise a hand
in their defence, but he had loved them well: his
smile had always welcomed their return.
They mourned for him unceasingly, refusing
to be comforted, as in the white winter day they
followed the deal shell that held his body to the
nameless grave by the little gray church.
They were his only mourners, these two
whom he had left friendless upon earth--the
young boy and the old dog.

"Surely, he will relent now and let the poor
lad come hither?" thought the miller's wife,
glancing at her husband smoking by the hearth.

Baas Cogez knew her thought, but he
hardened his heart, and would not unbar his
door as the little, humble funeral went by.

"The boy is a beggar," he said to himself: "he
shall not be about Alois."

The woman dared not say anything aloud,
but when the grave was closed and the mourners had gone, she put a wreath of immortelles
into Alois's hands and bade her go and lay it
reverently on the dark, unmarked mound where
the snow was displaced.

Nello and Patrasche went home with broken hearts. But even of that poor, melancholy,
cheerless home they were denied the consola-
tion.

There was a month's rent over-due for their
little home, and when Nello had paid the last
sad service to the dead he had not a coin left.

He went and begged grace of the owner of the hut, a cobbler who went every Sunday night to drink his pint of wine and smoke with Baas Cogez.

The cobbler would grant no mercy. He was a harsh, miserly man, and loved money. He claimed in default of his rent every stick and stone, every pot and pan, in the hut, and bade Nello and Patrasche be out of it on the morrow.

Now, the cabin was lowly enough, and in some sense miserable enough, and yet their hearts clove to it with a great affection. They had been so happy there, and in the summer, with its clambering vine and its flowering beans, it was so pretty and bright in the midst of the sunlighted fields!

There life in it had been full of labor and privation, and yet they had been so well content, so gay of heart, running together to meet the old man's never-failing smile of welcome!

애원하다 · (기한에 대한) 유예 기간 · 구두[신발] 수선공 · 매~, 모든 · 일요일 · 마시다 · 파인트(액량·건량 단위)

승인하다, 허락하다 · 자비 · 가혹한, 냉혹한구두쇠인, 수전노인 · 돈 · 채무 불이행 · 나무 막대기 · 돌멩이 · 냄비, 솥 · 프라이팬 · 오두막 · ~에서 떠나다[나가다] · 내일

오두막 · (중요도가) 낮은, 하찮은 · 비참한, 참담한, 처량한 · (무엇을 둘로) 쪼개다(cleave) · 애착, 애정 · 행복한 · 여름 · 기어오르는 · 포도넝쿨 · 콩 · 예쁜, 귀여운 · 밝은, 화사한 · 햇빛 비치는

~으로 가득한 · 육체노동 · 궁핍(=hardship) · 만족하다 · 즐거운, 명랑한 · 다함이 없는, 무진장한, 변하지 않는

All night long the boy and the dog sat by the fireless hearth in the darkness, drawn close together for warmth and sorrow.

불 없는, 불을 피우지 않은 / 어둠, 암측 / 끌다 / 가까이 / 온기, 따스함 / (큰) 슬픔, 비애(=grief)

Their bodies were insensible to the cold, but their hearts seemed frozen in them.

무감각한, (…을) 의식하지[알지] 못하는 / 얼어붙다

When the morning broke over the white, chill earth it was the morning of Christmas Eve.

아침이 밝아오다 / 쌀쌀한

With a shudder, Nello clasped close to him his only friend, while his tears fell hot and fast on the dog's frank forehead.

(공포추위 등으로) 몸을 떨다, (꽉) 껴안다 / 유일한 / 눈물 / 뜨거운 / 빠른 / 이마(=brow)

"Let us go, Patrasche--dear, dear Patrasche," he murmured. "We will not wait to be kicked out: let us go."

우리~하자 / 속삭이다, 소곤거리다, 중얼[웅얼]거리다 / 기다리다 / (발로) 차다

Patrasche had no will but his, and they went sadly, side by side, out from the little place which was so dear to them both, and in which every humble, homely thing was to them precious and beloved.

뜻, 의지 / 슬프게, 슬피 / 나란히 / 변변치 않은, 초라한 / 가정적인, 따뜻한 / 귀한, 소중한 / (대단히) 사랑하는

Patrasche drooped his head wearily as he passed by his own green cart: it was no longer

아래로 처지다[늘어지다] / 지쳐서; 녹초가 되어 / 지나가다 / ~곁을

his--it had to go with the rest to pay the rent, and his brass harness lay idle and glittering on the snow.

The dog could have lain down beside it and died for very heart-sickness as he went, but whilst the lad lived and needed him Patrasche would not yield and give way.

They took the old accustomed road into Antwerp. The day had yet scarce more than dawned, most of the shutters were still closed, but some of the villagers were about.

They took no notice whilst the dog and the boy passed by them.

At one door Nello paused and looked wistfully within: his grandfather had done many a kindly turn in neighbor's service to the people who dwelt there.

"Would you give Patrasche a crust?" he said, timidly. "He is old, and he has had nothing since last forenoon."

The woman shut the door hastily, murmur-
닫다 급히, 서둘러서, 허둥지둥
ing some vague saying about wheat and rye be-
모호한, 애매한 밀 호밀
ing very dear that season.
비싼, 귀한 계절

The boy and the dog went on again wearily:
지쳐서, 녹초가 되어
they asked no more.
요청하다 더 이상 ~아니다

By slow and painful ways they reached Ant-
천천히 고통스러운, 힘겨운 닿다, 도착하다
werp as the chimes tolled ten.
(차임벨) 소리 <종·시계가> 치다, <시각을> 알리다

"If I had anything about me I could sell
무엇이든, 아무거나 팔다
to get him bread!" thought Nello, but he had

nothing except the wisp of linen and serge that
아무것도 없는 ~외에는 조각 린넨 서지(짜임이 튼튼한 모직물)
covered him, and his pair of wooden shoes.
~을 덮다 쌍, 켤레 나무로 만든

Patrasche understood, and nestled his nose
이해하다 따뜻이 앉다[눕다] 코
into the lad's hand, as though to pray him not to
사내아이, 청년 기도하다
be disquieted for any woe or want of his.
불안해 하다, 동요하다 고민, 비통, 비애(=misery)

The winner of the drawing-prize was to be
승리자, 우승자 그림대회
proclaimed at noon, and to the public building
선언[선포]하다 (=declare) 정오 공회당 건물
where he had left his treasure Nello made his
놓다, 남겨두다 보물
way.

On the steps and in the entrance-hall there
계단 건물 입구
was a crowd of youths--some of his age, some
사람들, 군중, 무리 같은 나이 또래
older, all with parents or relatives or friends.
부모 친척 친구

His heart was sick with fear as he went
아픈, 병든　　　공포, 두려움
among them, holding Patrasche close to him.
~사이로, ~사이에서　꼭 붙잡다　　　　가까이
The great bells of the city clashed out the hour
도시　짱그랑거리다　　　시간, 시각
of noon with brazen clamor.
정오, 12시　뻔뻔한(=shameless)　아우성, 소란
The doors of the inner hall were opened; the
내부[안쪽]의, 중심부 가까이의
eager, panting throng rushed in: it was known
열렬한　가슴이 두근거리는 인파, 군중
that the selected picture would be raised above
선발된, 선택된　그림
the rest upon a wooden dais.
나무로 된　(방 한 쪽 끝에 만든) 연단
A mist obscured Nello's sight, his head
안개　보기[듣기/이해하기] 어렵게 하다　시야, 시력
swam, his limbs almost failed him.
(현기증이 나는 것처럼) 어질어질하다(swim)
When his vision cleared he saw the drawing
시력, 눈; 시야　　　　　그림
raised on high: it was not his own! A slow,
걸려 있는
sonorous voice was proclaiming aloud that
듣기 좋은, 낭랑한　　　선언[선포]하다(=declare)
victory had been adjudged to Stephen Kiessling-
승리, 우승　　　판단을 내리다, 판결하다
er, born in the burgh of Antwerp, son of a
태어나다　　자치구, 자치 도시
wharfinger in that town.
선창 주인[관리인]
When Nello recovered his consciousness he
(곤경 등을 벗어나 정상 상태로) 회복되다 자각, 의식
was lying on the stones without, and Patrasche
눕다
was trying with every art he knew to call him
시도하다　　　　　　　　기술
back to life.

In the distance a throng of the youths of
Antwerp were shouting around their successful
comrade, and escorting him with acclamations
to his home upon the quay.

The boy staggered to his feet and drew the
dog into his embrace.

"It is all over, dear Patrasche," he mur-
mured--"all over!"

He rallied himself as best he could, for he
was weak from fasting, and retraced his steps to
the village.

Patrasche paced by his side with his head
drooping and his old limbs feeble from hunger
and sorrow.

The snow was falling fast: a keen hurricane
blew from the north: it was bitter as death on
the plains.

It took them long to traverse the familiar
path, and the bells were sounding four of the
clock as they approached the hamlet.

Suddenly Patrasche paused, arrested by a
scent in the snow, scratched, whined, and drew
out with his teeth a small case of brown leather.
He held it up to Nello in the darkness.
Where they were there stood a little Calvary,
and a lamp burned dully under the cross: the
boy mechanically turned the case to the light:
on it was the name of Baas Cogez, and within it
were notes for two thousand francs.

The sight roused the lad a little from his
stupor. He thrust it in his shirt, and stroked Patrasche and drew him onward. The dog looked
up wistfully in his face.

Nello made straight for the mill-house, and
went to the house-door and struck on its panels.

The miller's wife opened it weeping, with
little Alois clinging close to her skirts.

"Is it thee, thou poor lad?" she said kindly
through her tears. "Get thee gone ere the Baas
see thee. We are in sore trouble to-night. He is
out seeking for a power of money that he has let

fall riding homeward, and in this snow he never will find it; and God knows it will go nigh to ruin us. It is Heaven's own judgment for the things we have done to thee."

Nello put the note-case in her hand and called Patrasche within the house.

"Patrasche found the money to-night," he said quickly. "Tell Baas Cogez so: I think he will not deny the dog shelter and food in his old age. Keep him from pursuing me, and I pray of you to be good to him."

Ere either woman or dog knew what he meant he had stooped and kissed Patrasche: then closed the door hurriedly, and disappeared in the gloom of the fast--falling night.

The woman and the child stood speechless with joy and fear: Patrasche vainly spent the fury of his anguish against the iron-bound oak of the barred house-door. They did not dare unbar the door and let him forth: they tried all they could to solace him.

They brought him sweet cakes and juicy meats; they tempted him with the best they had; they tried to lure him to abide by the warmth of the hearth; but it was of no avail.

Patrasche refused to be comforted or to stir from the barred portal.

It was six o'clock when from an opposite entrance the miller at last came, jaded and broken, into his wife's presence.

"It is lost forever," he said, with an ashen cheek and a quiver in his stern voice. "We have looked with lanterns everywhere: it is gone--the little maiden's portion and all!"

His wife put the money into his hand, and told him how it had come to her.

The strong man sank trembling into a seat and covered his face, ashamed and almost afraid.

"I have been cruel to the lad," he muttered at length: "I deserved not to have good at his hands."

Little Alois, taking courage, crept close to her father and nestled against him her fair curly head.

"Nello may come here again, father?" she whispered. "He may come to-morrow as he used to do?"

The miller pressed her in his arms: his hard, sunburned face was very pale and his mouth trembled.

"Surely, surely," he answered his child. "He shall bide here on Christmas Day, and any other day he will. God helping me, I will make amends to the boy--I will make amends."

Little Alois kissed him in gratitude and joy, then slid from his knees and ran to where the dog kept watch by the door.

"And to-night I may feast Patrasche?" she cried in a child's thoughtless glee.

Her father bent his head gravely: "Ay, ay: let the dog have the best;" for the stern old man was moved and shaken to his heart's depths.

It was Christmas Eve, and the mill-house
was filled with oak logs and squares of turf, with
~으로 가득 차다 / 통나무장작 / 정사각형 모양의 / 토탄
cream and honey, with meat and bread, and the
크림 / 꿀 / 고기
rafters were hung with wreaths of evergreen,
서까래 / 걸다, 매달다 / 리스, 화환 / 상록수
and the Calvary and the cuckoo clock looked
십자가상 / 뻐꾸기 시계
out from a mass of holly. There were little paper
덩어리[덩이] / 호랑가시나무 / 종이
lanterns, too, for Alois, and toys of various fash-
장난감 / 다양한, 여러 가지의
ions and sweetmeats in bright-pictured papers.
사탕, 설탕 절임한 것 / 반짝이는 그림이 그려진
There were light and warmth and abundance
밝은, 빛나는 / 온기, 따스함 / 풍부, 풍요
everywhere, and the child would fain have made
기꺼이, 흔쾌히
the dog a guest honored and feasted.
손님 / 명예로운, 귀한
But Patrasche would neither lie in the
~도 ~도 아닌
warmth nor share in the cheer. Famished he
나누다, 공유하다 / 즐거움, 명랑함
was and very cold, but without Nello he would
추운, 차가운 / ~없이
partake neither of comfort nor food.
먹다[마시다], 참가하다 / 안락함, 편안함 / 음식
Against all temptation he was proof, and
유혹(하는 것) / 맞서다, 견디다
close against the door he leaned always, watch-
기대다, 기대서다
ing only for a means of escape.
탈출, 도망
"He wants the lad," said Baas Cogez. "Good
원하다, 바라다
dog! good dog! I will go over to the lad the first
좋은, 착한
thing at day-dawn."
새벽, 동틀녘

For no one but Patrasche knew that Nello
알다
had left the hut, and no one but Patrasche
떠나다   오두막
divined that Nello had gone to face starvation
(직감으로) 알다, 예측하다   기아, 굶주림
and misery alone.
(심한) 고통
The mill-kitchen was very warm: great logs
방앗간 부엌   훈훈한, 따스한   통나무
crackled and flamed on the hearth; neighbors
탁탁 소리내다   활활 타오르다   난로
came in for a glass of wine and a slice of the fat
와인, 포도주   (얇게 썬) 조각
goose baking for supper.
거위   저녁 만찬
Alois, gleeful and sure of her playmate back
신이 난, 기쁜   소꿉동무
on the morrow, bounded and sang and tossed
내일   (신이 나서) 껑충껑충 달리다
back her yellow hair.

Baas Cogez, in the fulness of his heart,
충만함, 완벽함
smiled on her through moistened eyes, and
미소짓다   촉촉해진
spoke of the way in which he would befriend her
말하다   친구가 되어 주다
favorite companion; the house-mother sat with
가장 아끼는[사랑하는]
calm, contented face at the spinning-wheel; the
침착한, 차분한   만족한   물레
cuckoo in the clock chirped mirthful hours.
                짹짹[찍찍]거리다 유쾌한, 명랑한
Amidst it all Patrasche was bidden with a
명령하다(bid)
thousand words of welcome to tarry there a
지체하다 (=linger)
cherished guest. But neither peace nor plenty
소중히 여기다, 아끼다   평화   풍부, 풍요
could allure him where Nello was not.
마음을 끌다

88

When the supper smoked on the board, and the voices were loudest and gladdest, and the Christ-child brought choicest gifts to Alois, Patrasche, watching always an occasion, glided out when the door was unlatched by a careless new-comer, and as swiftly as his weak and tired limbs would bear him sped over the snow in the bitter, black night.

He had only one thought--to follow Nello. A human friend might have paused for the pleasant meal, the cheery warmth, the cosey slumber; but that was not the friendship of Patrasche.

He remembered a bygone time, when an old man and a little child had found him sick unto death in the wayside ditch.

Snow had fallen freshly all the evening long; it was now nearly ten; the trail of the boy's footsteps was almost obliterated.

It took Patrasche long to discover any scent. When at last he found it, it was lost again quickly, and lost and recovered, and again lost

and again recovered, a hundred times or more.
(100번도 더 넘게)

The night was very wild. The lamps under
(거친, 힘힌)

the wayside crosses were blown out; the roads
(길가, 도로변)

were sheets of ice; the impenetrable darkness
(넓게 퍼져 있는 것[층]) (들어갈[관통할] 수 없는, 눈앞이 안 보이는)

hid every trace of habitations; there was no liv-
(흔적, 자취) ((사람들이 사는) 거주지, 부락)

ing thing abroad.
(집 밖에)

All the cattle were housed, and in all the huts
((집합적으로) 소)

and homesteads men and women rejoiced and
((농장의 건물과 땅이 딸린) 주택[농가]) (대단히 기뻐하다)

feasted.
((아주 즐겁게) 맘껏 먹다)

There was only Patrasche out in the cruel
(잔인한, 혹독한)

cold--old and famished and full of pain, but with
(고통, 아픔)

the strength and the patience of a great love to
((역경을 견디는) 힘, 용기) (인내력, 인내심, 참을성)

sustain him in his search.
(살아가게[존재하게/지탱하게] 하다)

The trail of Nello's steps, faint and obscure
(자국, 흔적, 자취) (발걸음) (희미한) (이해하기 힘든, 모호한)

as it was under the new snow, went straightly
(~아래) (똑바로, 곧장)

along the accustomed tracks into Antwerp.
(익숙한)

It was past midnight when Patrasche traced
(자정, 12시)

it over the boundaries of the town and into the
(경계) (도시)

narrow, tortuous, gloomy streets.
(좁은) (구불구불한) (어둑어둑한, 음울한)

It was all quite dark in the town, save where
(꽤, 상당히, 몹시)

some light gleamed ruddily through the crev-
(어슴푸레[희미하게] 빛나다)

90

ices of house-shutters (덧문), or some group went homeward (집으로) with lanterns chanting drinking- (구호[성가]를 (거듭) 외치다[부르다]) songs.

The streets (거리, 도로) were all white (하얀) with ice (얼음): the high (높은) walls (벽, 담) and roofs (지붕) loomed (어렴풋이 나타나다, 흐릿하게 보이다) black against them. There was scarce (부족한, 드문) a sound save the riot (폭동) of the winds down the passages (통로, 길) as they tossed (던지다) the creaking (삐걱거리다) signs and shook the tall (키 큰) lamp-irons (가로등). So many passers-by (통행인, 나그네) had trodden (디디다, 밟다(tread)) through and through the snow, so many diverse (다양한) paths had crossed and recrossed (건너다; 가로지르다 재교차하다) each other (서로서로), that the dog had a hard task (일, 과업, 과제) to retain (유지하다) any hold on the track he followed.

But he kept on his way (계속 가다), though the cold pierced (뚫다[찌르다/박다]) him to the bone (뼈), and the jagged (뾰족뾰족한) ice cut his feet, and the hunger in his body gnawed (쏠다, 갉아먹다, 물어뜯다) like a rat's (쥐) teeth.

He kept on his way, a poor gaunt (수척한, 아주 야윈), shivering (부들부들 떨리는) thing, and by long patience (인내력, 인내심) traced the steps he loved into the very heart of the burgh (자치구, 자치 도시) and up to the steps of the great cathedral (대성당).

"He is gone to the things that he loved," thought Patrasche: he could not understand (이해하다), but he was full of sorrow and of pity for the art-passion that to him was so incomprehensible (이해할 수 없는, 이해하기 어려운) and yet so sacred (성스러운, 종교적인).

The portals (정문, 입구) of the cathedral were unclosed (닫지 않은) after the midnight mass (~뒤에 / 자정 미사). Some heedlessness (부주의함, 경솔함) in the custodians (관리인), too eager (열렬한) to go home and feast (연회, 만찬) or sleep, or too drowsy (졸리는(=sleepy)) to know whether (…이든 아니든) they turned (돌리다) the keys (열쇠) aright (제대로), had left one of the doors unlocked (잠기지 않다).

By that accident (우연, 사고) the foot-falls (발자국) Patrasche sought had passed through into the building, leaving the white (하얀색) marks (마크, 표시) of snow upon the dark (짙은, 어두운) stone floor (바닥).

By that slender (가느다란) white thread (실), frozen (얼어붙은, 결빙된) as it fell, he was guided (안내하다) through the intense (극심한, 강렬한) silence, through the immensity (임청남, 방대함) of the vaulted (아치형의, 천장[지붕]이 아치형의) space--guided straight to the gates (대문) of the chancel (성단소), and, stretched there upon the stones, he found Nello.

He crept up and touched the face of the boy.
creep의 과거, 과거분사　만지다, 손 대다　얼굴

"Didst thou dream that I should be faith-
충실하지 못한, 신뢰할 수 없는

less and forsake thee? I--a dog?" said that mute
저버리다　말없는

caress.
애무, 애정 표시

The lad raised himself with a low cry and
일어나다　낮은　울음

clasped him close.
(꽉) 껴안다

"Let us lie down and die together," he mur-
눕다　죽다　함께

mured. "Men have no need of us, and we are all
필요, 요구

alone."
혼자, 다른 사람 없이

In answer, Patrasche crept closer yet, and
대답　살금살금 움직이다

laid his head upon the young boy's breast. The
가슴, 흉부

great tears stood in his brown, sad eyes: not for
커다란　눈물　갈색의　슬픈

himself--for himself he was happy.
행복한

They lay close together in the piercing cold.
눕다　가까이　함께　날카로운, 꿰뚫는

The blasts that blew over the Flemish dikes
(훅 밀려드는 한 줄기의) 강한 바람　제방, 둑; 둑길

from the northern seas were like waves of ice,
북향의, 북부의　물결, 파도

which froze every living thing they touched.
얼리다, 얼게 하다　만지다, 닿다, 손 대다

The interior of the immense vault of stone
내부, 실내　어마어마한(=enormous) 둥근 천장이 있는 회랑

in which they were was even more bitterly chill
~조차, 심지어　혹독하게

than the snow-covered plains without.
눈으로 뒤덮인

Now and then a bat moved in the shadows-
때때로, 가끔 　박쥐 움직이다 　그늘, 어둠

-now and then a gleam of light came on the
어슴푸레한[흐릿한] 빛

ranks of carven figures. Under the Rubens they
조각한(carved). ~아래, ~밑에

lay together quite still, and soothed almost into
꽤, 아주 고요한, 정지한 (통증 등을) 누그러뜨리다[완화시키다]

a dreaming slumber by the numbing narcotic of
잠, 수면 마취약, 마약

the cold. Together they dreamed of the old glad
꿈꾸다 기쁜, 반가운

days when they had chased each other through
뒤쫓다, 추적하다

the flowering grasses of the summer meadows,
꽃이 핀[피어 있는] 여름 초원, 목초지

or sat hidden in the tall bulrushes by the water's
숨다, 숨기다 부들, 골풀 물가

side, watching the boats go seaward in the sun.
지켜보다 배 바다를 향한, 바다 방향의

Suddenly through the darkness a great white
갑자기, 별안간, 돌연 어둠 거대한, 위대한

radiance streamed through the vastness of the
빛, 광채, 광휘 줄줄[계속] 흐르다[흘러나오다] 광대(함), 광대한 넓이

aisles; the moon, that was at her height, had
통로 달 높이, 고도

broken through the clouds, the snow had ceased
깨뜨리다, 부수다 구름 중단되다, 그치다

to fall, the light reflected from the snow without
비추다, 반사하다

was clear as the light of dawn.
깨끗한, 선명한, 또렷한

It fell through the arches full upon the two

pictures above, from which the boy on his
그림 위에, 위로

entrance had flung back the veil: the Elevation
입장, 등장 내던지다(ling) 승진, 승격, 올라감

and the Descent of the Cross were for one in-
하강, 내려감 십자가 순간적으로

stant visible.
(눈에) 보이는, 알아볼 수 있는

Nello rose to his feet and stretched his
arms to them; the tears of a passionate ecstasy
glistened on the paleness of his face.

"I have seen them at last!" he cried aloud. "O
God, it is enough!"

His limbs failed under him, and he sank
upon his knees, still gazing upward at the
majesty that he adored.

For a few brief moments the light illumined
the divine visions that had been denied to him
so long--light clear and sweet and strong as
though it streamed from the throne of Heaven.

Then suddenly it passed away: once more a
great darkness covered the face of Christ.

The arms of the boy drew close again the
body of the dog.

"We shall see His face--_there,_" he murmured; "and He will not part us, I think."

On the morrow, by the chancel of the cathedral, the people of Antwerp found them both.

They were both dead: the cold of the night had
frozen into stillness alike the young life and the
old.

When the Christmas morning broke and the
priests came to the temple, they saw them lying
thus on the stones together.

Above the veils were drawn back from the
great visions of Rubens, and the fresh rays of
the sunrise touched the thorn-crowned head of
the Christ.

As the day grew on there came an old, hard-
featured man who wept as women weep.

"I was cruel to the lad," he muttered, "and
now I would have made amends--yea, to the
half of my substance--and he should have been
to me as a son."

There came also, as the day grew apace, a
painter who had fame in the world, and who
was liberal of hand and of spirit.

"I seek one who should have had the prize

yesterday had worth won," he said to the peo-

ple--"a boy of rare promise and genius. An old

wood-cutter on a fallen tree at eventide--that

was all his theme. But there was greatness for

the future in it. I would fain find him, and take

him with me and teach him Art."

And a little child with curling fair hair,

sobbing bitterly as she clung to her father's arm,

cried aloud.

"Oh, Nello, come! We have all ready for thee.

The Christ-child's hands are full of gifts, and the

old piper will play for us; and the mother says

thou shalt stay by the hearth and burn nuts with

us all the Noel week long--yes, even to the Feast

of the Kings! And Patrasche will be so happy!

Oh, Nello, wake and come!"

But the young pale face, turned upward to

the light of the great Rubens with a smile upon

its mouth, answered them all, "It is too late."

97

For the sweet, sonorous bells went ringing
달콤한   듣기 좋은, 낭랑한   울리다
through the frost, and the sunlight shone upon
서리, 성에   헷빛   비추다
the plains of snow, and the populace trooped
평원, 들판   대중들, 서민들   무리를 지어 가다
gay and glad through the streets, but Nello and
명랑한, 쾌활한   즐거운, 반가운   거리
Patrasche no more asked charity at their hands.
청하다   자비, 자선
All they needed now Antwerp gave unbidden.
요청[초대]받지 않은, 예상 밖의
Death had been more pitiful to them than
측은한, 가련한(=pathetic)
longer life would have been. It had taken the
one in the loyalty of love, and the other in the
충실, 충성
innocence of faith, from a world which for love
결백, 무죄, 천진   믿음, 신뢰, 신앙(심)
has no recompense and for faith no fulfilment.
보상, 배상   이행, 수행, 완수; 실천
All their lives they had been together, and
in their deaths they were not divided: for when
죽음   나누다, 가르다
they were found the arms of the boy were folded
감싸다, 둘러싸다
too closely around the dog to be severed without
가까이   극심한, 심각한
violence, and the people of their little village,
폭행, 폭력
contrite and ashamed, implored a special grace
깊이 뉘우치는, 회한에 찬   애원[간청]하다   특별한
for them, and, making them one grave, laid
무덤
them to rest there side by side--forever!
쉬다, 휴식하다   영원히

뉘른베르크의 난로

THE NÜRNBERG STOVE

THE NÜRNBERG STOVE

August lived in a little town called Hall.
아우구스트(남자 이름)   작은   (city보다 작은) (소)도시, 읍
Hall is a favorite name for several towns
할(마을 이름) 매우 좋아하는, 총애하는   여럿의, 수 개의, 몇몇의
in Austria and in Germany; but this one especial
오스트리아   독일   특별한
little Hall, in the Upper Innthal, is one of the
                    (어떤 것에서) 위쪽의[상부의]
most charming Old-World places that I know,
가장   매력적인, 멋진   옛날식의, 고풍스러운, 구시대의
and August for his part did not know any other.
                                              뭔가 다른 (것)
  It has the green meadows and the great
              초록의   초원, 목초지   커다란, 큰
mountains all about it, and the gray-green
(아주 높은) 산   회녹색
glacier-fed water rushes by it.
빙하에서 공급된   급(속)히 움직이다, 돌진하다
  It has paved streets and enchanting little
      (널돌·벽돌 능으로) 포장하디   황홀케 하는(=delightful)
shops that have all latticed panes and iron grat-
가게, 상점   격자, 격자 모양의   쇠
ings to them.

It has a very grand old Gothic church, that
웅장한, 장려한 / 고딕 양식의

has the noblest blendings of light and shadow,
가장 고결한[고귀한] / 혼합, 융합, 조합 / 그림자

and marble tombs of dead knights, and a look of
대리석 / 무덤 / 죽은 / 기사

infinite strength and repose as a church should
한계가 없는, 무한한 / 힘 / 휴식, 수면, 안식

have.

Then there is the Muntze Tower, black and
화폐 주조소 / 탑 / 검은색

white, rising out of greenery and looking down
흰색, 하양 / …의 밖으로 / 녹색 나뭇잎[화초], 푸른잎, 녹지

on a long wooden bridge and the broad rapid
나무로 만든 / 다리 / (폭이) 넓은 / (속도가) 빠른

river.
강

And there is an old schloss which has been
성(castle), 궁전(palace)

made into a guard-house, with battlements and
(군대의) 위병소, 영창 / 총안(銃眼)이 있는 흉벽

frescos and heraldic devices in gold and colors,
프레스코화[화법] / 의전(관)의, 문장(紋章)의 / 장치, 기구

and a man-at-arms carved in stone standing
(중세의) 중기병(重騎兵) / 조각하다, 깎아서 만들다

life-size in his niche and bearing his date 1530.
실물 크기의 / 벽감(壁龕) / (벽이나 기둥 같은) 지지물

A little farther on, but close at hand, is a
더 멀리, 더 먼 / 쉽게 손닿는[갈 수 있는] 곳에

cloister with beautiful marble columns and
수도원, 수녀원 / 아름다운 / 대리석의 / 기둥[원주], 기념비

tombs, and a colossal wood-carved Calvary, and
무덤 / 거대한, 엄청난 / 그리스도 수난상, 십자가상

beside that a small and very rich chapel.
~옆에 / 소예배당, 분회당

Indeed, so full is the little town of the
정말로, 실제로 / ~이 그득한[아주 많은]

undisturbed past, that to walk in it is like
누구의 방해도 받지 않는 / 걷다

opening a missal of the Middle Ages, all
열다, 펼치다   (가톨릭의) 미사전서[기도서]   중세 시대
emblazoned and illuminated with saints and
선명히 새겨진[장식된]   채색한, 채식한   성인, 성자
warriors, and it is so clean, and so still, and
전사(戰士)   깨끗한, 청결한   고요한, 조용한
so noble, by reason of its monuments and its
고상한, 고귀한   기념비적인[역사적인] 건축물
historic color, that I marvel much no one has
역사적인   경탄하다
ever cared to sing its praises.
칭찬, 찬사, 찬양
The old pious heroic life of an age at once
경건한, 독실한
more restful and more brave than ours still
편안한, 평화로운   용기 있는, 용감한
leaves its spirit there, and then there is the
정신, 영혼
girdle of the mountains all around, and that
둘러싸는 것, 테두리   모든   사방에(서), 빙 둘러
alone means strength, peace, majesty.
혼자 (힘으로), 단독으로   평화   장엄함, 위풍당당함
In this little town a few years ago August
어느 정도, 조금(a little)
Strehla lived with his people in the stone-paved
~와 함께 살다   가족   돌로 포장된
irregular square where the grand church stands.
고르지[가지런하지] 못한, 불규칙적인   웅장한   서다

He was a small boy of nine years at that
작은, 조그만   9세, 아홉 살   그 당시
time,—a chubby-faced little man with rosy
통통한, 토실토실한   장밋빛
cheeks, big hazel eyes, and clusters of curls the
녹갈색[적갈색]인   무리, 다발   곱슬곱슬한 머리카락
brown of ripe nuts.
익은, 숙성한
His mother was dead, his father was poor,
어머니   죽은   아버지   가난한
and there were many mouths at home to feed.
입   밥[우유]을 먹이다

In this country the winters are long and very
국가, 지역, 고장   겨울   긴   매우, 몹시
cold, the whole land lies wrapped in snow for
추운, 차가운   전체의   땅, 뭍, 나라 싸다, 둘러싸다 눈
many months, and this night that he was trot-
달, 개월   밤(중)   빨리 걷다, 속보로 가다
ting home, with a jug of beer in his numb red
        (손잡이가 달린) 주전자[병] (추위 등으로) 감각이 없는
hands, was terribly cold and dreary.
        끔찍하게, 혹독하게   음울한, 따분한 (=dull)

The good burghers of Hall had shut their
        (특정 소도시의) 시민[주민]   닫다
double shutters, and the few lamps there were
이중의   덧문, 셔터   약간의, 몇 개의
flickered dully behind their quaint, old-fash-
깜박거리다 둔하게, 지루하게; 느리게 진기한, 예스러운
ioned iron casings.
        싸개, 포장

The mountains indeed were beautiful, all
                정말로, 실제로   아름다운
snow-white under the stars that are so big in
        ~아래, ~밑에   별   큰, 커다란
frost.
성에, 서리

Hardly any one was astir; a few good souls
거의...아니다[없다]   움직이다   영혼, 정신
wending home from vespers, a tired post-boy
(천천히) 가다[이동하다]   저녁 기도[예배]의 지친, 피곤한 우편배달부 소년
who blew a shrill blast from his tasselled horn as
        불다 새된, 날카로운 빵[삑] 하는 소리 술(tassel)을 달아 장식한
he pulled up his sledge before a hostelry, and lit-
                썰매   호텔, 여관, 여인숙
tle August hugging his jug of beer to his ragged
        (무엇을) 끌어안다   누더기가 된, 다 해진
sheepskin coat, were all who were abroad, for
양가죽   집 밖에
the snow fell heavily and the good folks of Hall
        (양·정도가) 심하게[아주 많이] (일반적인) 사람들
go early to their beds.
    일찍

He could not run, or he would have spilled
the beer; he was half frozen and a little frightened, but he kept up his courage by saying over
and over again to himself, "I shall soon be at
home with dear Hirschvogel."

He went on through the streets, past the
stone man-at-arms of the guard-house, and so
into the place where the great church was, and
where near it stood his father Karl Strehla's
house, with a sculptured Bethlehem over the
door-way, and the Pilgrimage of the Three Kings
painted on its wall.

He had been sent on a long errand outside
the gates in the afternoon, over the frozen fields
and the broad white snow, and had been be-
lated, and had thought he had heard the wolves
behind him at every step, and had reached the
town in a great state of terror, thankful with all
his little panting heart to see the oil-lamp burning under the first house-shrine.

But he had not forgotten to call for the beer,
잊다(forget) ~을 요구하다 맥주

and he carried it carefully now, though his
나르다, 운반하다 조심스럽게, 주의 깊게 비록 ~지만

hands were so numb that he was afraid they
(추위 등으로 신체 부위가) 감각이 없는

would let the jug down every moment.
순간, 잠깐

The snow outlined with white every gable
윤곽을 보여주다[나타내다] 박공, 합각

and cornice of the beautiful old wooden hous-
(장식용) 처마[천장] 돌림띠 나무로 된, 목조의

es; the moonlight shone on the gilded signs,
달빛 비추다 금박을 입힌, 도금을 한

the lambs, the grapes, the eagles, and all the
어린[새끼] 양 포도 독수리

quaint devices that hung before the doors;
진기한, 예스러운 장치, 기구

covered lamps burned before the Nativities and
덮다 불타다 예수의 탄생[성탄]

Crucifixions painted on the walls or let into the
십자가에 못 박힌 예수를 그린 그림 벽, 담

wood-work; here and there, where a shutter
여기저기에(서) 덧문, 셔터

had not been closed, a ruddy fire-light lit up a
닫다 붉은, 불그스름한 light

homely interior, with the noisy band of children
(자기 집처럼) 아늑한[편안한] 시끄러운, 떠들썩한

clustering round the house-mother and a big
무리를 이루다, (소규모로) 모이다

brown loaf, or some gossips spinning and lis-
빵 한 덩이 소문, 험담 돌리다, 회전시키다

tening to the cobbler's or the barber's story of
구두[신발] 수선공 이발사

a neighbor, while the oil-wicks glimmered, and
이웃(사람) (기름등잔의) 심지 (희미하게) 깜박이다[빛나다]

the hearth-logs blazed, and the chestnuts sput-
난로 속 통나무[장작] 활활 타다 밤 탁탁 소리를 내다

tered in their iron roasting-pot.
쇠, 철 구이용 냄비

Little August saw all these things, as he saw
보다(see)
everything with his two big bright eyes that had
모든 것   큰, 커다란   반짝이는
such curious lights and shadows in them; but
궁금한, 호기심이 많은 (=inquisitive)
he went heedfully on his way for the sake of the
주의 깊게, 조심스럽게   ~ 때문에, ~를 위해
beer which a single slip of the foot would make
미끄러짐, (작은) 실수
him spill.
흐르다, 쏟아지다; 흘리다, 쏟다
At his knock and call the solid oak door,
두드리다, 노크하다(=rap)   단단한, 견고한
four centuries old if one, flew open, and the boy
4세기, 400년   낳다(fly)
darted in with his beer, and shouted, with all the
쏜살같이[휙] 달리다[움직이다]   크게 소리치다, 고함을 지르다
force of mirthful lungs, "Oh, dear Hirschvogel,
유쾌한, 명랑한   폐, 허파
but for the thought of you I should have died!"
생각   죽다

It was a large barren room into which he
척박한, 황량한
rushed with so much pleasure, and the bricks
돌진하다, 달려들다   기쁨, 즐거움   벽돌
were bare and uneven.
벌거벗은, 맨–   평평하지 않은, 울퉁불퉁한
It had a walnut-wood press, handsome
호두나무   (커다란) 장(欌)   보기 좋은, 멋진
and very old, a broad deal table, and several
넓은   전나무 재목의   여럿의, 몇몇의
wooden stools for all its furniture; but at the top
의자, 스툴   가구
of the chamber, sending out warmth and color
(특정 목적용) -실(室)   온기   색깔
together as the lamp shed its rays upon it, was a
함께   (빛을) 발하다   광선, 선, 빛살
tower of porcelain, burnished with all the hues
자기(磁器)

106

of a king's peacock and a queen's jewels, and
surmounted with armed figures, and shields,
and flowers of heraldry, and a great golden
crown upon the highest summit of all.

It was a stove of 1532, and on it were the
letters H. R. H., for it was in every portion the
handwork of the great potter of Nürnberg, Augustin Hirschvogel, who put his mark thus, as
all the world knows.

The stove no doubt had stood in palaces and
been made for princes, had warmed the crimson
stockings of cardinals and the gold-broidered
shoes of archduchesses, had glowed in presence
-chambers and lent its carbon to help kindle
sharp brains in anxious councils of state; no one
knew what it had seen or done or been fashioned for; but it was a right royal thing.

Yet perhaps it had never been more use-
ful than it was now in this poor desolate room,
sending down heat and comfort into the troop
of children tumbled together on a wolf-skin

at its feet, who received frozen August among
them with loud shouts of joy.

"Oh, dear Hirschvogel, I am so cold, so cold!"
said August, kissing its gilded lion's claws. "Is
father not in, Dorothea?"

"No, dear. He is late."

Dorothea was a girl of seventeen, dark-
haired and serious, and with a sweet sad face,
for she had had many cares laid on her shoulders, even whilst still a mere baby.
She was the eldest of the Strehla family; and
there were ten of them in all.
Next to her there came Jan and Karl and
Otho, big lads, gaining a little for their own living; and then came August, who went up in the
summer to the high alps with the farmers' cattle,
but in winter could do nothing to fill his own
little platter and pot.
And then all the little ones, who could only

open their mouths to be fed like young birds,—
Albrecht and Hilda, and Waldo and Christof,
and last of all little three-year-old Ermengilda,
with eyes like forget-me-nots, whose birth had
cost them the life of their mother.

They were of that mixed race, half Austrian,
half Italian, so common in the Tyrol; some of
the children were white and golden as lilies,
others were brown and brilliant as fresh-fallen
chestnuts.

The father was a good man, but weak and
weary with so many to find for and so little to
do it with. He worked at the salt-furnaces, and
by that gained a few florins; people said he
would have worked better and kept his family
more easily if he had not loved his pipe and a
draught of ale too well; but this had only been
said of him after his wife's death, when trouble
and perplexity had begun to dull a brain never
too vigorous, and to enfeeble further a character
already too yielding.

As it was, the wolf often bayed at the door of the Strehla household, without a wolf from the mountains coming down.

Dorothea was one of those maidens who almost work miracles, so far can their industry and care and intelligence make a home sweet and wholesome and a single loaf seem to swell into twenty.

The children were always clean and happy, and the table was seldom without its big pot of soup once a day. Still, very poor they were, and Dorothea's heart ached with shame, for she knew that their father's debts were many for flour and meat and clothing.

Of fuel to feed the big stove they had always enough without cost, for their mother's father was alive, and sold wood and fir cones and coke, and never grudged them to his grandchildren, though he grumbled at Strehla's improvidence and hapless, dreamy ways.

"Father says we are never to wait for him:

we will have supper, now you have come home, dear," said Dorothea, who, however she might fret her soul in secret as she knitted their hose and mended their shirts, never let her anxieties cast a gloom on the children.

Only to August she did speak a little sometimes, because he was so thoughtful and so tender of her always, and knew as well as she did that there were troubles about money,— though these troubles were vague to them both, and the debtors were patient and kindly, being neighbors all in the old twisting streets between the guard-house and the river.

Supper was a huge bowl of soup, with big slices of brown bread swimming in it and some onions bobbing up and down: the bowl was soon emptied by ten wooden spoons. And then the three eldest boys slipped off to bed, being tired with their rough bodily la-bor in the snow all day, and Dorothea drew her spinning-wheel by the stove and set it whirring,

and the little ones got August down upon the
old worn wolf-skin and clamored to him for a
picture or a story. For August was the artist of
the family.

He had a piece of planed deal that his father
had given him, and some sticks of charcoal, and
he would draw a hundred things he had seen in
the day, sweeping each out with his elbow when
the children had seen enough of it and sketching
another in its stead,—faces and dogs' heads, and
men in sledges, and old women in their furs,
and pine-trees, and cocks and hens, and all sorts
of animals, and now and then—very reverently—
a Madonna and Child.

It was all very rough, for there was no one to
teach him anything.

But it was all life-like, and kept the whole
troop of children shrieking with laughter, or
watching breathless, with wide open, wondering, awed eyes.

They were all so happy: what did they care

for the snow outside? Their little bodies were warm, and their hearts merry; even Dorothea, troubled about the bread for the morrow, laughed as she spun; and August, with all his soul in his work, and little rosy Ermengilda's cheek on his shoulder, glowing after his frozen afternoon, cried out loud, smiling, as he looked up at the stove that was shedding its heat down on them all,—

"Oh, dear Hirschvogel! you are almost as great and good as the sun! No; you are greater and better, I think, because he goes away no-body knows where all these long, dark, cold hours, and does not care how people die for want of him; but you—you are always ready: just a little bit of wood to feed you, and you will make a summer for us all the winter through!"

The grand old stove seemed to smile through all its iridescent surface at the praises of the child. No doubt the stove, though it had known

three centuries and more, had known but very
3세기, 300년
little gratitude.
고마움, 감사, 사의

It was one of those magnificent stoves in
참으로 아름다운[감명 깊은], 으리으리한
enamelled faïence which so excited the jealousy
에나멜[도료]을 입힌 파이앙스 도자기((채색을 한 프랑스 도기   질투[시기], 시샘
of the other potters of Nürnberg that in a body
도예가, 도공
they demanded of the magistracy that Augus-
요구하다; 강력히 묻다, 따지다   치안 판사들
tin Hirschvogel should be forbidden to make
금(지)하다, ~을 못하게 하다
any more of them,—the magistracy, happily,

proving of a broader mind, and having no
입증[증명]하다   (폭이) 넓은
sympathy with the wish of the artisans to crip-
동정, 연민   소원, 의도, 소망   장인, 기능 보유자(=craftsman)
ple their greater fellow. It was of great height
높이
and breadth, with all the majolica lustre which
폭, 너비   마욜리카 도자기(이탈리아산 화려한 도자기)
Hirschvogel learned to give to his enamels when

he was making love to the young Venetian girl
베네치아의 소녀
whom he afterwards married.
나중에, 그 뒤에

There was the statue of a king at each cor-
조각상   각각의
ner, modelled with as much force and splendor
모델로 하다   힘   화려함, 장려함
as his friend Albrecht Dürer could have given
알브레히트 뒤러(독일의 화가이자 판화가)
unto them on copperplate or canvas.
동판

The body of the stove itself was divided into
몸, 본체   나누다
panels, which had the Ages of Man painted on
(사각형) 판   (생애의 특정) 시기

them in polychrome; the borders of the panels had roses and holly and laurel and other foliage, and German mottoes in black letter of odd Old-World moralizing, such as the old Teutons, and the Dutch after them, love to have on their chimney-places and their drinking-cups, their dishes and flagons.

The whole was burnished with gilding in many parts, and was radiant everywhere with that brilliant coloring of which the Hirschvogel family, painters on glass and great in chemistry as they were, were all masters.

The stove was a very grand thing, as I say: possibly Hirschvogel had made it for some mighty lord of the Tyrol at that time when he was an imperial guest at Innsbruck and fashioned so many things for the Schloss Amras and beautiful Philippine Welser, the burgher's daughter, who gained an archduke's heart by her beauty and the right to wear his honors by her wit.

Nothing was known of the stove at this latter day in Hall. The grandfather Strehla, who had been a master-mason, had dug it up out of some ruins where he was building, and, finding it without a flaw, had taken it home, and only thought it worth finding because it was such a good one to burn.

That was now sixty years past, and ever since then the stove had stood in the big desolate empty room, warming three generations of the Strehla family, and having seen nothing prettier perhaps in all its many years than the children tumbled now in a cluster like gathered flowers at its feet.

For the Strehla children, born to nothing else, were all born with beauty: white or brown, they were equally lovely to look upon, and when they went into the church to mass, with their curling locks and their clasped hands, they stood under the grim statues like cherubs flown down off some fresco.

"Tell us a story, August," they cried, in chorus, when they had seen charcoal pictures till they were tired; and August did as he did every night pretty nearly,—looked up at the stove and told them what he imagined of the many adventures and joys and sorrows of the human being who figured on the panels from his cradle to his grave.

To the children the stove was a household god. In summer they laid a mat of fresh moss all round it, and dressed it up with green boughs and the numberless beautiful wild flowers of the Tyrol country.

In winter all their joys centred in it, and scampering home from school over the ice and snow they were happy, knowing that they would

soon be cracking nuts or roasting chestnuts in the broad ardent glow of its noble tower, which rose eight feet high above them with all its spires and pinnacles and crowns.

Once a travelling peddler had told them that

the letters on it meant Augustin Hirschvogel,
and that Hirschvogel had been a great German

potter and painter, like his father before him,
in the art-sanctified city of Nürnberg, and had
made many such stoves, that were all miracles
of beauty and of workmanship, putting all his
heart and his soul and his faith into his labors,
as the men of those earlier ages did, and thinking but little of gold or praise.

An old trader too, who sold curiosities not
far from the church, had told August a little
more about the brave family of Hirschvogel,
whose houses can be seen in Nürnberg to this
day; of old Veit, the first of them, who painted
the Gothic windows of St. Sebald with the mar-
riage of the Margravine; of his sons and of his
grandsons, potters, painters, engravers all, and
chief of them great Augustin, the Luca della
Robbia of the North.

And August's imagination, always quick, had
made a living personage out of these few records,

and saw Hirschvogel as though he were in the flesh walking up and down the Maximilian-Strass in his visit to Innsbruck, and maturing beautiful things in his brain as he stood on the bridge and gazed on the emerald-green flood of the Inn.

So the stove had got to be called Hirschvogel in the family, as if it were a living creature, and little August was very proud because he had been named after that famous old dead German who had had the genius to make so glorious a thing.

All the children loved the stove, but with August the love of it was a passion; and in his secret heart he used to say to himself, "When I am a man, I will make just such things too, and then I will set Hirschvogel in a beautiful room in a house that I will build myself in Innsbruck just outside the gates, where the chestnuts are, by the river: that is what I will do when I am a man."

For August, a salt-baker's son and a little cow-keeper when he was anything, was a dreamer of dreams, and when he was upon the high alps with his cattle, with the stillness and the sky around him, was quite certain that he would live for greater things than driving the herds up when the spring-tide came among the blue sea of gentians, or toiling down in the town with wood and with timber as his father and grandfather did every day of their lives.

He was a strong and healthy little fellow, fed on the free mountain-air, and he was very happy, and loved his family devotedly, and was as active as a squirrel and as playful as a hare; but he kept his thoughts to himself, and some of them went a very long way for a little boy who was only one among many, and to whom no-body had ever paid any attention except to teach him his letters and tell him to fear God. August in winter was only a little, hungry school-boy, trotting to be catechised by the

120

priest, or to bring the loaves from the bake-
house, or to carry his father's boots to the cobbler; and in summer he was only one of hundreds of cow-boys, who drove the poor, half-
blind, blinking, stumbling cattle, ringing their
throat-bells, out into the sweet intoxication of
the sudden sunlight, and lived up with them in
the heights among the Alpine roses, with only
the clouds and the snow-summits near.

But he was always thinking, thinking, thinking, for all that; and under his little sheepskin
winter coat and his rough hempen summer
shirt his heart had as much courage in it as
Hofer's ever had,—great Hofer, who is a house-
hold word in all the Innthal, and whom August
always reverently remembered when he went to
the city of Innsbruck and ran out by the foaming
water-mill and under the wooded height of Berg
Isel.

August lay now in the warmth of the stove
and told the children stories, his own little

brown face growing red with excitement as his imagination glowed to fever-heat.

That human being on the panels, who was drawn there as a baby in a cradle, as a boy play-ing among flowers, as a lover sighing under a casement, as a soldier in the midst of strife, as a father with children round him, as a weary, old, blind man on crutches, and, lastly, as a ransomed soul raised up by angels, had always had the most intense interest for August, and he had made, not one history for him, but a thou-sand; he seldom told them the same tale twice.

He had never seen a story-book in his life; his primer and his mass-book were all the volumes he had.

But nature had given him Fancy, and she is a good fairy that makes up for the want of very many things! only, alas! her wings are so very soon broken, poor thing, and then she is of no use at all.

"It is time for you all to go to bed, children," said Dorothea, looking up from her spinning. "Father is very late to-night; you must not sit up for him."

"Oh, five minutes more, dear Dorothea!" they pleaded; and little rosy and golden Er-mengilda climbed up into her lap.

"Hirschvogel is so warm, the beds are never so warm as he. Cannot you tell us another tale, August?"

"No," cried August, whose face had lost its light, now that his story had come to an end, and who sat serious, with his hands clasped on his knees, gazing on to the luminous arabesques of the stove.

"It is only a week to Christmas," he said, suddenly.

"Grandmother's big cakes!" chuckled little Christof, who was five years old, and thought Christmas meant a big cake and nothing else.

"What will Santa Claus find for 'Gilda if she

be good?" murmured Dorothea over the child's sunny head; for, however hard poverty might pinch, it could never pinch so tightly that Dorothea would not find some wooden toy and some rosy apples to put in her little sister's socks.

"Father Max has promised me a big goose, because I saved the calf's life in June," said August; it was the twentieth time he had told them so that month, he was so proud of it.

"And Aunt Maïla will be sure to send us wine and honey and a barrel of flour; she always does," said Albrecht.

Their aunt Maïla had a chalet and a little farm over on the green slopes towards Dorp Ampas.

"I shall go up into the woods and get Hirschvogel's crown," said August; they always crowned Hirschvogel for Christmas with pine boughs and ivy and mountain-berries.

The heat soon withered the crown; but it was

part of the religion of the day to them, as much
(종교와도 같은 것, (개인의 삶에서) 아주 중요한 것)
so as it was to cross themselves in church and
raise their voices in the "O Salutaris Hostia."
(목소리를 높이다) (오 살루타리스 호스티아(엘가르가 작곡한 성가))
And they fell chatting of all they would do on
(담소[이야기]를 나누다, 수다를 떨다)
the Christ-night, and one little voice piped loud
(높은 소리로 말하다)
against another's, and they were as happy as
(~에 맞서, ~에 대항하여)
though their stockings would be full of golden
(~으로 가득 차다)
purses and jewelled toys, and the big goose in
((작은) 지갑) (보석이 박힌) (거위)
the soup-pot seemed to them such a meal as
(수프 냄비) (식사, 끼니)
kings would envy.
(부러워하다, 선망하다)
In the midst of their chatter and laughter a
(중앙, 한가운데(=middle))
blast of frozen air and a spray of driven snow
((훅 밀려드는 한 줄기의) 강한 바람[공기]) (물보라, 비말)
struck like ice through the room, and reached
(닿다, 도달하다)
them even in the warmth of the old wolf-skins
(따스함, 훈기) (늑대 가죽)
and the great stove.

It was the door which had opened and let
(문) (열다)
in the cold; it was their father who had come
home.

The younger children ran joyous to meet
(아주 기뻐하는; 기쁜)
him. Dorothea pushed the one wooden arm-
(밀다) (나무로 만든 팔걸이 의자)
chair of the room to the stove, and August flew

to set the jug of beer on a little round table, and
fill a long clay pipe; for their father was good to
them all, and seldom raised his voice in anger,
and they had been trained by the mother they
had loved to dutifulness and obedience and a
watchful affection.

To-night Karl Strehla responded very
wearily to the young ones' welcome, and came
to the wooden chair with a tired step and sat
down heavily, not noticing either pipe or beer.

"Are you not well, dear father?" his daughter
asked him.

"I am well enough," he answered, dully, and
sat there with his head bent, letting the lighted
pipe grow cold.

He was a fair, tall man, gray before his time,
and bowed with labor.

"Take the children to bed," he said, suddenly, at last, and Dorothea obeyed. August stayed
behind, curled before the stove; at nine years
old, and when one earns money in the summer

from the farmers, one is not altogether a child
any more, at least in one's own estimation.

August did not heed his father's silence: he
was used to it. Karl Strehla was a man of few
words, and, being of weakly health, was usually
too tired at the end of the day to do more than
drink his beer and sleep.

August lay on the wolf-skin, dreamy and
comfortable, looking up through his drooping
eyelids at the golden coronets on the crest of
the great stove, and wondering for the millionth
time whom it had been made for, and what
grand places and scenes it had known.

Dorothea came down from putting the little
ones in their beds; the cuckoo-clock in the corner struck eight; she looked to her father and
the untouched pipe, then sat down to her spinning, saying nothing.

She thought he had been drinking in some
tavern; it had been often so with him of late.

There was a long silence; the cuckoo called

the quarter twice; August dropped asleep, his
curls falling over his face; Dorothea's wheel
hummed like a cat.

Suddenly Karl Strehla struck his hand on the
table, sending the pipe on the ground.

"I have sold Hirschvogel," he said; and his
voice was husky and ashamed in his throat. The
spinning-wheel stopped. August sprang erect
out of his sleep.

"Sold Hirschvogel!"

If their father had dashed the holy crucifix
on the floor at their feet and spat on it, they
could not have shuddered under the horror of a
greater blasphemy.

"I have sold Hirschvogel!" said Karl Strehla,
in the same husky, dogged voice.

"I have sold it to a travelling trader in such
things for two hundred florins. What would
you?—I owe double that. He saw it this morning
when you were all out. He will pack it and take
it to Munich to-morrow."

Dorothea gave a low shrill cry:

"Oh, father!—the children—in mid-winter!"

She turned white as the snow without; her words died away in her throat.

August stood, half blind with sleep, staring with dazed eyes as his cattle stared at the sun when they came out from their winter's prison.

"It is not true! It is not true!" he muttered.

"You are jesting, father?"

Strehla broke into a dreary laugh.

"It is true. Would you like to know what is true too?—that the bread you eat, and the meat you put in this pot, and the roof you have over your heads, are none of them paid for, have been none of them paid for for months and months: if it had not been for your grandfather I should have been in prison all summer and autumn, and he is out of patience and will do no more now. There is no work to be had; the masters go to younger men: they say I work ill; it may be so. Who can keep his head above

129

water with ten hungry children dragging him down? When your mother lived, it was different. Boy, you stare at me as if I were a mad dog! You have made a god of yon china thing. Well—it goes: goes to-morrow. Two hundred florins, that is something. It will keep me out of prison for a little, and with the spring things may turn——"

August stood like a creature paralyzed. His eyes were wide open, fastened on his father's with terror and incredulous horror; his face had grown as white as his sister's; his chest heaved with tearless sobs.

"It is not true! It is not true!" he echoed, stupidly. It seemed to him that the very skies must fall, and the earth perish, if they could take away Hirschvogel. They might as soon talk of tearing down God's sun out of the heavens.

"You will find it true," said his father, doggedly, and angered because he was in his own soul bitterly ashamed to have bartered away the heirloom and treasure of his race and the comfort and health-giver of his young children.

"You will find it true. The dealer has paid me half the money to-night, and will pay me the other half to-morrow when he packs it up and takes it away to Munich. No doubt it is worth a great deal more,—at least I suppose so, as he gives that,—but beggars cannot be choosers. The little black stove in the kitchen will warm you all just as well. Who would keep a gilded, painted thing in a poor house like this, when one can make two hundred florins by it? Dorothea, you never sobbed more when your mother died. What is it, when all is said?—a bit of hardware much too grand-looking for such a room as this. If all the Strehlas had not been born fools it would have been sold a century ago, when it was dug up out of the ground. 'It is a stove for a museum,' the trader said when he saw it. To a museum let it go."

August gave a shrill shriek like a hare's when it is caught for its death, and threw himself on his knees at his father's feet.

"Oh, father, father!" he cried, convulsively, his hands closing on Strehla's knees, and his uplifted face blanched and distorted with terror. "Oh, father, dear father, you cannot mean what you say? Send it away—our life, our sun, our joy, our comfort? We shall all die in the dark and the cold. Sell me rather. Sell me to any trade or any pain you like; I will not mind. But Hirschvogel!—it is like selling the very cross off the altar! You must be in jest. You could not do such a thing—you could not!—you who have always been gentle and good, and who have sat in the warmth here year after year with our mother. It is not a piece of hardware, as you say; it is a living thing, for a great man's thoughts and fancies have put life into it, and it loves us though we are only poor little children, and we love it with all our hearts and souls, and up in

132

heaven I am sure the dead Hirschvogel knows!

Oh, listen; I will go and try and get work to-
시도하다   얻다, 갖다
morrow! There must be something I could do,
어떤 것
and I will beg the people we owe money to to
빌다, 애원하다   빚지다
wait; they are all neighbors, they will be patient.
기다리다   이웃   인내심이 있는
But sell Hirschvogel!—oh, never! never! never!

Give the florins back to the vile man. Tell him it
극도로 불쾌한[나쁜]
would be like selling the shroud out of mother's
수의(壽衣)
coffin! Oh, father, dear father! do hear me, for
관   듣다
pity's sake!"
제발, 아무쪼록, 제발 (부탁인데), 가엾게 여기시고

Strehla was moved by the boy's anguish. He
가슴[마음]이 뭉클해지게[아프게] 하 (극심한) 괴로움, 비통
loved his children, though he was often weary
자주, 흔히   지친, 피곤한
of them, and their pain was pain to him. But
고통, 통증, 아픔
besides emotion, and stronger than emotion,
감정, 정서   더 강한, 더 힘센
was the anger that August roused in him: he
화, 분노   (어떤 감정을) 불러일으키다
hated and despised himself for the barter of the
미워[증오]하다 경멸하다   물건을 교환하다
heirloom of his race, and every word of the child
(집안의) 가보   혈족, 일족; 가계
stung him with a stinging sense of shame.
쏘다, 찌르다(STING의 과거·과거분사)   수치심, 창피, 부끄러움
And he spoke in his wrath rather than in his
(극도의) 분노, 노여움
sorrow.
슬픔, 비탄

"You are a little fool," he said, harshly, as they had never heard him speak. "You rave like a play-actor. Get up and go to bed. The stove is sold. There is no more to be said. Children like you have nothing to do with such matters. The stove is sold, and goes to Munich to-morrow. What is it to you? Be thankful I can get bread for you. Get on your legs, I say, and go to bed."

Strehla took up the jug of ale as he paused, and drained it slowly as a man who had no cares.

August sprang to his feet and threw his hair back off his face; the blood rushed into his cheeks, making them scarlet; his great soft eyes flamed alight with furious passion.

"You dare not!" he cried, aloud, "you dare not sell it, I say! It is not yours alone; it is ours——"

Strehla flung the emptied jug on the bricks with a force that shivered it to atoms, and, rising to his feet, struck his son a blow that felled him

to the floor. It was the first time in all his life
마루   첫 번째
that he had ever raised his hand against any one
                 돌리다, 들다
of his children.

Then he took the oil-lamp that stood at his
                            석유등잔
elbow and stumbled off to his own chamber
팔꿈치   비틀거리다, 휘청거리다   방
with a cloud before his eyes.
        구름

"What has happened?" said August, a little
while later, as he opened his eyes and saw Dorothea weeping above him on the wolf-skin before
the stove. He had been struck backward, and
his head had fallen on the hard bricks where the
wolf-skin did not reach. He sat up a moment,
with his face bent upon his hands.

"I remember now," he said, very low, under
his breath.

Dorothea showered kisses on him, while her
tears fell like rain.

"But, oh, dear, how could you speak so to father?" she murmured. "It was very wrong."

"No, I was right," said August, and his little
mouth, that hitherto had only curled in laughter, curved downward with a fixed and bitter
seriousness.

"How dare he? How dare he?" he muttered,
with his head sunk in his hands. "It is not his
alone. It belongs to us all. It is as much yours
and mine as it is his."

Dorothea could only sob in answer. She was too frightened to speak. The authority of their parents in the house had never in her remembrance been questioned.

"Are you hurt by the fall, dear August?" she murmured, at length, for he looked to her so pale and strange.

"Yes—no. I do not know. What does it matter?"

He sat up upon the wolf-skin with passionate pain upon his face; all his soul was in rebellion, and he was only a child and was powerless.

"It is a sin; it is a theft; it is an infamy," he said, slowly, his eyes fastened on the gilded feet of Hirschvogel.

"Oh, August, do not say such things of father!" sobbed his sister. "Whatever he does, we ought to think it right."

August laughed aloud.

"Is it right that he should spend his money in drink?—that he should let orders lie unexecuted?—that he should do his work so ill that no one cares to employ him?—that he should live on grandfather's charity, and then dare sell a thing that is ours every whit as much as it is his? To sell Hirschvogel! Oh, dear God! I would sooner sell my soul!"

"August!" cried Dorothea, with piteous entreaty. He terrified her, she could not recognize her little, gay, gentle brother in those fierce and blasphemous words.

August laughed aloud again; then all at once his laughter broke down into bitterest weeping. He threw himself forward on the stove, covering it with kisses, and sobbing as though his heart would burst from his bosom.

What could he do? Nothing, nothing, nothing!

"August, dear August," whispered Dorothea, piteously, and trembling all over,—for she was a very gentle girl, and fierce feeling terrified her,—"August, do not lie there. Come to bed: it is quite late. In the morning you will be calmer. It is horrible indeed, and we shall die of cold, at least the little ones; but if it be father's will——"

"Let me alone," said August, through his teeth, striving to still the storm of sobs that shook him from head to foot. "Let me alone. In the morning!—how can you speak of the morning?"

"Come to bed, dear," sighed his sister. "Oh, August, do not lie and look like that! you frighten me. Do come to bed."

"I shall stay here."

"Here! all night!"

"They might take it in the night. Besides, to leave it now!"

"But it is cold! the fire is out."

"It will never be warm any more, nor shall we."

All his childhood had gone out of him, all his gleeful, careless, sunny temper had gone with it; he spoke sullenly and wearily, choking down the great sobs in his chest. To him it was as if the end of the world had come.

His sister lingered by him while striving to persuade him to go to his place in the little crowded bedchamber with Albrecht and Waldo and Christof. But it was in vain.

"I shall stay here," was all he answered her.

And he stayed,—all the night long.

The lamps went out; the rats came and ran across the floor; as the hours crept on through midnight and past, the cold intensified and the air of the room grew like ice. August did not move; he lay with his face downward on the golden and rainbow-hued pedestal of the house-hold treasure, which henceforth was to be cold for evermore, an exiled thing in a foreign city in a far-off land.

Whilst yet it was dark his three elder broth-ers came down the stairs and let themselves out, each bearing his lantern and going to his work in stone-yard and timber-yard and at the salt-

works. They did not notice him; they did not
know what had happened.

A little later his sister came down with a light
in her hand to make ready the house ere morning should break.

She stole up to him and laid her hand on his
shoulder timidly.

"Dear August, you must be frozen. August,
do look up! do speak!"

August raised his eyes with a wild, feverish,
sullen look in them that she had never seen
there. His face was ashen white: his lips were
like fire.

He had not slept all night; but his passionate
sobs had given way to delirious waking dreams
and numb senseless trances, which had
alternated one on another all through the
freezing, lonely, horrible hours.

"It will never be warm again," he muttered,
"never again!"

Dorothea clasped him with trembling hands.

"August! do you not know me?" she cried, in an agony. "I am Dorothea. Wake up, dear—wake up! It is morning, only so dark!"

August shuddered all over.

"The morning!" he echoed.

He slowly rose up on to his feet.

"I will go to grandfather," he said, very low.

"He is always good: perhaps he could save it."

Loud blows with the heavy iron knocker of the house-door drowned his words. A strange voice called aloud through the keyhole,—

"Let me in! Quick!—there is no time to lose! More snow like this, and the roads will all be blocked. Let me in! Do you hear? I am come to take the great stove."

August sprang erect, his fists doubled, his eyes blazing.

"You shall never touch it!" he screamed; "you shall never touch it!"

"Who shall prevent us?" laughed a big man,

143

who was a Bavarian, amused at the fierce little figure fronting him.

"I!" said August. "You shall never have it! you shall kill me first!"

"Strehla," said the big man, as August's father entered the room, "you have got a little mad dog here: muzzle him."

One way and another they did muzzle him. He fought like a little demon, and hit out right and left, and one of his blows gave the Bavarian a black eye.

But he was soon mastered by four grown men, and his father flung him with no light hand out from the door of the back entrance, and the buyers of the stately and beautiful stove set to work to pack it heedfully and carry it away.

When Dorothea stole out to look for August, he was nowhere in sight. She went back to little 'Gilda, who was ailing, and sobbed over the child, whilst the others stood looking on, dimly understanding that with Hirschvogel was going all the warmth of their bodies, all the light of their hearth.

Even their father now was sorry and ashamed; but two hundred florins seemed a big sum to him, and, after all, he thought the children could warm themselves quite as well at the black iron stove in the kitchen. Besides, whether he regretted it now or not, the work of the Nürnberg potter was sold irrevocably, and he had to stand still and see the men from Munich wrap it in manifold wrappings and bear it out into the snowy air to where an ox-cart stood in waiting for it. In another moment Hirschvogel was gone,—gone forever and aye.

August had stood still for a time, leaning, sick and faint from the violence that had been used to him, against the back wall of the house. The wall looked on a court where a well was, and the backs of other houses, and beyond them the spire of the Muntze Tower and the peaks of the mountains.

Into the court an old neighbor hobbled for water, and, seeing the boy, said to him,—

"Child, is it true your father is selling the big painted stove?"

August nodded his head, then burst into a passion of tears.

"Well, for sure he is a fool," said the neighbor. "Heaven forgive me for calling him so before his own child! but the stove was worth a mint of money. I do remember in my young days, in old Anton's time (that was your great-grandfather, my lad), a stranger from Vienna saw it, and said that it was worth its weight in gold."

August's sobs went on their broken, impetuous course.

"I loved it! I loved it!" he moaned. "I do not care what its value was. I loved it! I loved it!"

"You little simpleton!" said the old man, kindly. "But you are wiser than your father, when all's said. If sell it he must, he should have taken it to good Herr Steiner over at Sprüz, who would have given him honest value. But no doubt they took him over his beer,—ay, ay! but if I were you I would do better than cry. I would go after it."

August raised his head, the tears raining down his cheeks.

"Go after it when you are bigger," said the neighbor, with a good-natured wish to cheer him up a little. "The world is a small thing after all: I was a travelling clockmaker once upon a time, and I know that your stove will be safe enough whoever gets it; anything that can be sold for a round sum is always wrapped up in cotton wool by everybody. Ay, ay, don't cry so much; you will see your stove again some day."

Then the old man hobbled away to draw his brazen pail full of water at the well.

August remained leaning against the wall; his head was buzzing and his heart fluttering with the new idea which had presented itself to his mind. "Go after it," had said the old man.

He thought, "Why not go with it?"

He loved it better than any one, even better

than Dorothea; and he shrank from the thought

of meeting his father again, his father who had

sold Hirschvogel.

He was by this time in that state of exaltation

in which the impossible looks quite natural and

commonplace. His tears were still wet on his

pale cheeks, but they had ceased to fall.

He ran out of the court-yard by a little gate,

and across to the huge Gothic porch of the

church. From there he could watch unseen his

father's house-door, at which were always hang-

ing some blue-and-gray pitchers, such as are

common and so picturesque in Austria, for a

part of the house was let to a man who dealt in

pottery.

He hid himself in the grand portico, which

he had so often passed through to go to mass

or complin within, and presently his heart gave

a great leap, for he saw the straw-enwrapped stove brought out and laid with infinite care on the bullock-dray.

Two of the Bavarian men mounted beside it, and the sleigh-wagon slowly crept over the snow of the place,—snow crisp and hard as stone. The noble old minster looked its grandest and most solemn, with its dark-gray stone and its vast archways, and its porch that was itself as big as many a church, and its strange gargoyles and lamp-irons black against the snow on its roof and on the pavement; but for once August had no eyes for it: he only watched for his old friend. Then he, a little unnoticeable figure enough, like a score of other boys in Hall, crept, unseen by any of his brothers or sisters, out of the porch and over the shelving uneven square, and followed in the wake of the dray.

Its course lay towards the station of the railway, which is close to the salt-works, whose smoke at times sullies this part of clean little

Hall, though it does not do very much damage.

From Hall the iron road runs northward through glorious country to Salzburg, Vienna, Prague, Buda, and southward over the Brenner into Italy. Was Hirschvogel going north or south? This at least he would soon know.

August had often hung about the little station, watching the trains come and go and dive into the heart of the hills and vanish.

No one said anything to him for idling about; people are kind-hearted and easy of temper in this pleasant land, and children and dogs are both happy there.

He heard the Bavarians arguing and vociferating a great deal, and learned that they meant to go too and wanted to go with the great stove itself. But this they could not do, for neither could the stove go by a passenger-train nor they themselves go in a goods-train.

So at length they insured their precious burden for a large sum, and consented to send it by

a luggage-train which was to pass through Hall
in half an hour. The swift trains seldom deign to
notice the existence of Hall at all.

August heard, and a desperate resolve made
itself up in his little mind. Where Hirschvogel
went would he go. He gave one terrible thought
to Dorothea—poor, gentle Dorothea!—sitting in
the cold at home, then set to work to execute his
project.

How he managed it he never knew very
clearly himself, but certain it is that when the
goods-train from the north, that had come all
the way from Linz on the Danube, moved out of
Hall, August was hidden behind the stove in the
great covered truck, and wedged, unseen and
undreamt of by any human creature, amidst the
cases of wood-carving, of clocks and clock-work,
of Vienna toys, of Turkish carpets, of Russian
skins, of Hungarian wines, which shared the
same abode as did his swathed and bound
Hirschvogel.

No doubt he was very naughty, but it never
occurred to him that he was so: his whole mind
and soul were absorbed in the one entrancing
idea, to follow his beloved friend and fire-king.

It was very dark in the closed truck, which
had only a little window above the door; and it
was crowded, and had a strong smell in it from
the Russian hides and the hams that were in it.

But August was not frightened; he was close
to Hirschvogel, and presently he meant to be

closer still; for he meant to do nothing less than
get inside Hirschvogel itself.

Being a shrewd little boy, and having had by
great luck two silver groschen in his breeches-
pocket, which he had earned the day before by
chopping wood, he had bought some bread and
sausage at the station of a woman there who
knew him, and who he was going out to
his uncle Joachim's chalet above Jenbach.

This he had with him, and this he ate in the
darkness and the lumbering, pounding, thun-

dering noise which made him giddy, as never
had he been in a train of any kind before.

Still he ate, having had no breakfast, and
being a child, and half a German, and not knowing at all how or when he ever would eat again.
When he had eaten, not as much as he wanted,
but as much as he thought was prudent (for who
could say when he would be able to buy anything more?), he set to work like a little mouse
to make a hole in the withes of straw and hay
which enveloped the stove.

If it had been put in a packing-case he would
have been defeated at the onset. As it was, he
gnawed, and nibbled, and pulled, and pushed,
just as a mouse would have done, making his
hole where he guessed that the opening of the
stove was,—the opening through which he had
so often thrust the big oak logs to feed it.
No one disturbed him; the heavy train went
lumbering on and on, and he saw nothing at all
of the beautiful mountains, and shining waters,

and great forests through which he was being
carried.

He was hard at work getting through the
straw and hay and twisted ropes; and get
through them at last he did, and found the door
of the stove, which he knew so well, and which
was quite large enough for a child of his age
to slip through, and it was this which he had
counted upon doing.

Slip through he did, as he had often done at
home for fun, and curled himself up there to see
if he could anyhow remain during many hours.
He found that he could; air came in through
the brass fret-work of the stove; and with ad-
mirable caution in such a little fellow he leaned
out, drew the hay and straw together, and rear-
ranged the ropes, so that no one could ever have
dreamed a little mouse had been at them.
Then he curled himself up again, this time
more like a dormouse than anything else; and,
being safe inside his dear Hirschvogel and

intensely cold, he went fast asleep as if he were
in his own bed at home with Albrecht and
Christof on either side of him.

The train lumbered on, stopping often and long, as the habit of goods-trains is, sweeping the snow away with its cow-switcher, and rumbling through the deep heart of the mountains, with its lamps aglow like the eyes of a dog in a night of frost. The train rolled on in its heavy, slow fashion, and the child slept soundly for a long while. When he did awake, it was quite dark outside in the land; he could not see, and of course he was in absolute darkness; and for a while he was sorely frightened, and trembled terribly, and sobbed in a quiet heart-broken fashion, thinking of them all at home.

Poor Dorothea! how anxious she would be! How she would run over the town and walk up to grandfather's at Dorf Ampas, and perhaps even send over to Jenbach, thinking he had taken refuge with Uncle Joachim!

몹시, 격하게 · 깊이[곤히] 잠들다 · 마치 ~인 것처럼 · 양쪽 · (육중한 덩치로) 느릿느릿 움직이다 · 자주 · 오래, 길게 · 버릇, 습관 · 쓸다, 털다, 청소하다 · 교환기, 전환기 · 덜거덕거리며 가다 · 환히 빛나는 · 숲, 삼림 · 구르다, 굴러가다 · 무거운, 육중한 · 깊이, 곤히 · 오랫동안, 한참 동안 · 잠에서 깨다 · 꽤, 상당히 · 바깥, ~밖 · 완전한, 완벽한 · 어둠, 암흑 · 몹시, 심하게 · (몸을) 떨다 · 극심하게, 지독하게 · 흐느끼다 · 조용한, 고요한 · 가련한, 불쌍한 · 불안해하는, 염려하는 · 아마, 어쩌면 · 보내다 · 피신(처), 도피(처)

His conscience smote him for the sorrow he
must be even then causing to his gentle sister;
but it never occurred to him to try and go back.
If he once were to lose sight of Hirschvogel
how could he ever hope to find it again? how
could he ever know whither it had gone,—north,
south, east, or west?

The old neighbor had said that the world
was small; but August knew at least that it must
have a great many places in it: that he had seen
himself on the maps on his school-house walls.

Almost any other little boy would, I think,
have been frightened out of his wits at the position in which he found himself; but August was
brave, and he had a firm belief that God and
Hirschvogel would take care of him.

The master-potter of Nürnberg was always
present to his mind, a kindly, benign, and
gracious spirit, dwelling manifestly in that porcelain tower whereof he had been the maker.

A droll fancy, you say? But every child with
a soul in him has quite as quaint fancies as this
one was of August's.

So he got over his terror and his sobbing
both, though he was so utterly in the dark. He
did not feel cramped at all, because the stove
was so large, and air he had in plenty, as it came
through the fret-work running round the top.
He was hungry again, and again nibbled
with prudence at his loaf and his sausage. He
could not at all tell the hour. Every time the
train stopped and he heard the banging, stamp-
ing, shouting, and jangling of chains that went
on, his heart seemed to jump up into his mouth.

If they should find him out! Sometimes porters came and took away this case and the other,
a sack here, a bale there, now a big bag, now a
dead chamois. Every time the men trampled
near him, and swore at each other, and banged
this and that to and fro, he was so frightened
that his very breath seemed to stop.

When they came to lift the stove out, would they find him? and if they did find him, would they kill him? That was what he kept thinking of all the way, all through the dark hours, which seemed without end.

The goods-trains are usually very slow, and are many days doing what a quick train does in a few hours. This one was quicker than most, because it was bearing goods to the King of Bavaria; still it took all the short winter's day and the long winter's night and half another day to go over ground that the mail-trains cover in a forenoon.

It passed great armored Kuffstein standing across the beautiful and solemn gorge, denying the right of way to all the foes of Austria.

It passed twelve hours later, after lying by in out-of-the-way stations, pretty Rosenheim, that marks the border of Bavaria.

And here the Nürnberg stove, with August inside it, was lifted out heedfully and set under a covered way. When it was lifted out (들어올리다), the boy had hard work to keep in his screams (비명); he was tossed (던지다) to and fro (앞뒤로) as the men lifted the huge (거대한) thing, and the earthenware (도기의, 도자기의) walls of his beloved (무척 사랑하는) fire-king were not cushions (쿠션) of down ((새의) 솜털).

However (어쨌든, 하지만), though they swore and grumbled (욕하다 / 투덜[툴툴]거리다) at the weight (무게) of it, they never suspected (수상쩍어[의심쩍어] 하다) that a living child (살아 있는) was inside it, and they carried it out (나르다, 운반하다) on to the platform ((기차역의) 플랫폼, 승강장) and set it down under the roof (지붕) of the goods-shed (화물 창고).

There it passed the rest (나머지) of the night and all the next morning, and August was all the while (다음(의)) within it.

The winds (바람) of early (이른, 일찍) winter sweep bitterly (휘몰아치다 / 혹독하게, 지독하게) over Rosenheim, and all the vast (광대한, 엄청나게 넓은) Bavarian plain (평원, 들판) was one white sheet of snow. If there had not been whole armies (부대, 집단(특정 목적을 위한 사람들)) of men at work always (늘, 항상) clearing (청소하는) the iron rails (철길, 철로) of the snow, no trains (기차) could ever have run at all.

Happily (다행히, 행복하게) for August, the thick wrappings (두꺼운 / 포장) in which the stove was enveloped (감싸다, 뒤덮다) and the stout- (튼튼함.)

ness of its own make screened him from the cold, of which, else, he must have died,—frozen.

He had still some of his loaf, and a little—a very little—of his sausage. What he did begin to suffer from was thirst; and this frightened him almost mere than anything else, for Dorothea had read aloud to them one night a story of the tortures some wrecked men had endured be- cause they could not find any water but the salt sea. It was many hours since he had last taken a drink from the wooden spout of their old pump, which brought them the sparkling, ice-cold wa- ter of the hills.

But, fortunately for him, the stove, hav- ing been marked and registered as "fragile and valuable," was not treated quite like a mere bale of goods, and the Rosenheim station-master, who knew its consignees, resolved to send it on by a passenger-train that would leave there at daybreak.

And when this train went out, in it, among
piles of luggage belonging to other travellers, to
무더기, 더미　화물, 짐　　~ 소유[것]이다, ~에 속하다　　여행자, 여행객
Vienna, Prague, Buda-Pest, Salzburg, was Au-
빈, 비엔나　　프라하　　부다페스트　　잘츠부르크
gust, still undiscovered, still doubled up like a
발견되지 않다, 들키지 않다　　두 겹이 되게 하다[접다]
mole in the winter under the grass.
두더지　　　　　　~아래, ~밑에

Those words, "fragile and valuable," had
단어, 낱말
made the men lift Hirschvogel gently and with
들다, 들어올리다　　　　부드럽게　　조심스럽게
care. He had begun to get used to his prison,
~에 익숙해지다　　감옥, 감방
and a little used to the incessant pounding and
끊임없는, 쉴새없는　쿵쾅거리는 소리
jumbling and rattling and shaking with which
뒤죽박죽 섞이는 것　　덜거덕[덜컹]거리는　흔들리는
modern travel is always accompanied, though
현대의, 근대의, 현대적인, 모던한　　동반하다, 동행하다
modern invention does deem itself so mightily
발명품　　　　　　(…로) 여기다[생각하다]
clever.

All in the dark he was, and he was terribly
어둠, 암흑　　　　　　　몹시, 극심하게, 지독히
thirsty; but he kept feeling the earthenware
목이 마른, 갈증이 나는　　　　　　도자기
sides of the Nürnberg giant and saying, softly,
거인
"Take care of me; oh, take care of me, dear
~을 보살피다[돌보다/신경 쓰다]
Hirschvogel!"

He did not say, "Take me back;" for, now
돌려보내다
that he was fairly out in the world, he wished to
바라다
see a little of it.

He began to think that they must have
been all over the world in all this time that the
전체에 걸쳐, 전체적으로
rolling and roaring and hissing and jangling
구르다, 굴러가다   으르렁거리다[포효하다] 쉬익 소리를 내다   땡그렁]거리다
had been about his ears shut up in the dark, he
began to remember all the tales that had been
기억하다, 떠올리다   이야기, 동화
told in Yule round the fire at his grandfather's
크리스마스(고어)
good house at Dorf, of gnomes and elves and
땅속 요정   요정, 엘프
subterranean terrors, and the Erl King riding
지하(세계)의   공포의 내상, 두려운[무서운] 존재   ~을 타다
on the black horse of night, and—and—and he
검은 말, 흑마
began to sob and to tremble again, and this time
흐느끼다   (몸을) 떨다, 떨리다
did scream outright.
비명(을 지르다)   노골적으로, 드러내 놓고
But the steam was screaming itself so loudly
증기   날카롭게 외치는, 쇳소리를 지르는; 삑삑 우는
that no one, had there been any one nigh, would
가까이
have heard him; and in another minute or so the
train stopped with a jar and a jerk, and he in his
삐걱거리는 소리 홱 움직임
cage could hear men crying aloud, "München!
새장
München!"

Then he knew enough of geography to know
지리학, (한 지역의) 지리[지형]
that he was in the heart of Bavaria. He had had
심장
an uncle killed in the Bayerischenwald by the
삼촌   죽다   바이에른 숲
Bavarian forest guards, when in the excitement
삼림 경비대   흥분, 신남

of hunting a black bear he had overpassed the
limits of the Tyrol frontier.

That fate of his kinsman, a gallant young
chamois-hunter who had taught him to handle
a trigger and load a muzzle, made the very name
of Bavaria a terror to August.

"It is Bavaria! It is Bavaria!" he sobbed to the
stove; but the stove said nothing to him; it had
no fire in it.

A stove can no more speak without fire than
a man can see without light. Give it fire, and it
will sing to you, tell tales to you, offer you in return all the sympathy you ask.

"It is Bavaria!" sobbed August; for it is always a name of dread augury to the Tyroleans,
by reason of those bitter struggles and midnight
shots and untimely deaths which come from
those meetings of jäger and hunter in the Bayerischenwald.

But the train stopped; Munich was reached,
and August, hot and cold by turns, and shaking

like a little aspen-leaf, felt himself once more
carried out on the shoulders of men, rolled
along on a truck, and finally set down, where
he knew not, only he knew he was thirsty,—so
thirsty! If only he could have reached his hand
out and scooped up a little snow!

He thought he had been moved on this truck
many miles, but in truth the stove had been only
taken from the railway-station to a shop in the
Marienplatz.

Fortunately, the stove was always set upright
on its four gilded feet, an injunction to that ef-
fect having been affixed to its written label, and
on its gilded feet it stood now in the small dark
curiosity-shop of one Hans Rhilfer.

"I shall not unpack it till Anton comes," he
heard a man's voice say; and then he heard a
key grate in a lock, and by the unbroken stillness
that ensued he concluded he was alone, and
ventured to peep through the straw and hay.
What he saw was a small square room filled

with pots and pans, pictures, carvings, old blue
냄비   프라이팬 그림   조각품
jugs, old steel armor, shields, daggers, Chinese
물병   강철   갑옷   방패   검   중국의
idols, Vienna china, Turkish rugs, and all the art
(신으로 숭배되는) 우상   도자기   카펫, 양탄자
lumber and fabricated rubbish of a bric-à-brac
잡동사니   직물[천]으로 된   (질이) 형편없는 것, 쓰레기 (같은 것)
dealer's.

It seemed a wonderful place to him; but, oh!
          놀라운, 감탄스러운, 굉장한
was there one drop of water in it all? That was
                방울
his single thought; for his tongue was parching,
단 하나의, 유일한   혀, 혓바닥   바싹 마른
and his throat felt on fire, and his chest began to
        목구멍   가슴
be dry and choked as with dust.
          숨이 막히다, 질식할 지경이다
There was not a drop of water, but there was

a lattice window grated, and beyond the window
격자창   ~뒤에
was a wide stone ledge covered with snow.
        널찍한   (창문 아래 벽에 붙인) 선반
August cast one look at the locked door,
          시선을 던지다   잠긴
darted out of his hiding-place, ran and opened
쏜살같이[휙] 달리다   숨어 있던 곳, 은신처
the window, crammed the snow into his mouth
              밀어[쑤셔] 넣다
again and again, and then flew back into the
계속해서
stove, drew the hay and straw over the place he

entered by, tied the cords, and shut the brass
들어가다   묶다   닫다   황동의
door down on himself.

He had brought some big icicles in with him,
and by them his thirst was finally, if only tempo-
rarily, quenched. Then he sat still in the bottom
of the stove, listening intently, wide awake, and
once more recovering his natural boldness.

The thought of Dorothea kept nipping his
heart and his conscience with a hard squeeze
now and then; but he thought to himself.

"If I can take her back Hirschvogel, then
how pleased she will be, and how little 'Gilda
will clap her hands!"

He was not at all selfish in his love for
Hirschvogel: he wanted it for them all at home
quite as much as for himself.

There was at the bottom of his mind a kind of ache of shame that his father—his own father—should have stripped their hearth and sold their honor thus.

A robin had been perched upon a stone griffin sculptured on a house-eave near. August had felt for the crumbs of his loaf in his pocket, and had thrown them to the little bird sitting so easily on the frozen snow.

In the darkness where he was he now heard a little song, made faint by the stove-wall and the window-glass that was between him and it, but still distinct and exquisitely sweet. It was the robin, singing after feeding on the crumbs.

August, as he heard, burst into tears. He thought of Dorothea, who every morning threw out some grain or some bread on the snow before the church.

"What use is it going there," she said, "if we forget the sweetest creatures God has made?"

Poor Dorothea! Poor, good, tender, much-burdened little soul! He thought of her till his tears ran like rain.

Yet it never once occurred to him to dream of going home. Hirschvogel was here.

Presently the key turned in the lock of the door; he heard heavy footsteps and the voice of the man who had said to his father, "You have a little mad dog; muzzle him!"

The voice said, "Ay, ay, you have called me a fool many times. Now you shall see what I have gotten for two hundred dirty florins. Potztausend! never did you do such a stroke of work."

Then the other voice grumbled and swore, and the steps of the two men approached more closely, and the heart of the child went pit-a-pat, pit-a-pat, as a mouse's does when it is on the top of a cheese and hears a housemaid's broom sweeping near.

They began to strip the stove of its wrappings: that he could tell by the noise they made
with the hay and the straw.

Soon they had stripped it wholly: that,
too, he knew by the oaths and exclamations of
wonder and surprise and rapture which broke
from the man who had not seen it before.

"A right royal thing! A wonderful and nev-
er-to-be-rivalled thing! Grander than the great
stove of Hohen-Salzburg! Sublime! magnificent!
matchless!"
So the epithets ran on in thick guttural voices, diffusing a smell of lager-beer so strong as
they spoke that it reached August crouching in
his stronghold.

If they should open the door of the stove!

That was his frantic fear. If they should open
it, it would be all over with him. They would
drag him out; most likely they would kill him,
he thought, as his mother's young brother had
been killed in the Wald.

The perspiration rolled off his forehead
땀(=sweat)   굴러 떨어지다   이마
in his agony; but he had control enough over
극도의 (육체적·정신적) 고통[괴로움]   조절하다, 통제하다
himself to keep quiet, and after standing by the
조용한, 고요한
Nürnberg master's work for nigh an hour, prais-
칭찬하다
ing, marvelling, expatiating in the lengthy Ger-
경이로워하다, 경탄하다 상세히 설명하다
man tongue, the men moved to a little distance
언어   움직이다, 이동하다   먼 곳[지점]
and began talking of sums of money and divided
합계, 총액, 금액
profits, of which discourse he could make out no
이익, 수익, 이윤   담론, 담화
meaning.

All he could make out was that the name of
~을 이해하다[알다], 알아듣다
the king—the king—the king came over very often in their arguments. He fancied at times they
논쟁; 언쟁, 말다툼   생각[상상]하다
quarrelled, for they swore lustily and their voic-
다투다, 언쟁을 벌이다, 싸우다   활기차게
es rose hoarse and high; but after a while they
(목) 쉰   잠시 뒤에
seemed to pacify each other and agree to some-
(화가 난 사람을) 진정시키다[달래다] (=placate)
thing, and were in great glee, and so in these
신이 남
merry spirits came and slapped the luminous
즐거운   (손바닥으로) 철썩 때리다[치다]
sides of stately Hirschvogel, and shouted to it,
소리치다
"Old Mumchance, you have brought us rare
말이 없는, 말이 없이, 무언의, 무언으로.   진귀한
good luck! To think you were smoking in a silly
fool of a salt-baker's kitchen all these years!"
제염소 일꾼   부엌

171

Then inside the stove August jumped up, with flaming cheeks and clinching hands, and was almost on the point of shouting out to them that they were the thieves and should say no evil of his father, when he remembered, just in time, that to breathe a word or make a sound was to bring ruin on himself and sever him forever from Hirschvogel.

So he kept quite still, and the men barred the shutters of the little lattice and went out by the door, double-locking it after them. He had made out from their talk that they were going to show Hirschvogel to some great person: therefore he kept quite still and dared not move.

Muffled sounds came to him through the shutters from the streets below,—the rolling of wheels, the clanging of church-bells, and bursts of that military music which is so seldom silent in the streets of Munich.

An hour perhaps passed by; sounds of steps on the stairs kept him in perpetual apprehension. In the intensity of his anxiety, he forgot that he was hungry and many miles away from cheerful, Old World little Hall, lying by the clear gray river-water, with the ramparts of the mountains all around.

Presently the door opened again sharply. He could hear the two dealers' voices murmuring unctuous words, in which "honor," "gratitude," and many fine long noble titles played the chief parts.

The voice of another person, more clear and refined than theirs, answered them curtly, and then, close by the Nürnberg stove and the boy's ear, ejaculated a single "Wunderschön!"

August almost lost his terror for himself in his thrill of pride at his beloved Hirschvogel be-ing thus admired in the great city. He thought the master-potter must be glad too.

"Wunderschön!" ejaculated the stranger a second time, and then examined the stove in all its parts, read all its mottoes, gazed long on all its devices.

"It must have been made for the Emperor Maximilian," he said at last; and the poor little boy, meanwhile, within, was "hugged up into nothing," as you children say, dreading that every moment he would open the stove.

And open it truly he did, and examined the brass-work of the door; but inside it was so dark that crouching August passed unnoticed, screwed up into a ball like a hedgehog as he was.

The gentleman shut to the door at length, without having seen anything strange inside it; and then he talked long and low with the tradesmen, and, as his accent was different from that which August was used to, the child could distinguish little that he said, except the name of the king and the word "gulden" again and again.

After a while he went away, one of the deal-ers accompanying him, one of them lingering behind to bar up the shutters. Then this one also withdrew again, double-locking the door.

The poor little hedgehog uncurled itself and dared to breathe aloud.

What time was it? Late in the day, he thought, for to accompany the stranger they had lighted a lamp; he had heard the scratch of the match, and through the brass fret-work had seen the lines of light. He would have to pass the night here, that was certain. He and Hirschvogel were locked in, but at least they were together. If only he could have had something to eat! He thought with a pang of how at this hour at home they ate the sweet soup, sometimes with apples in it from Aunt Maïla's farm orchard, and sang together, and listened to Dorothea's read-ing of little tales, and basked in the glow and delight that had beamed on them from the great Nürnberg fire-king.

"Oh, poor, poor little 'Gilda! What is she doing without the dear Hirschvogel?" he thought.
Poor little 'Gilda! she had only now the black
iron stove of the ugly little kitchen. Oh, how
cruel of father!

August could not bear to hear the dealers
blame or laugh at his father, but he did feel that
it had been so, so cruel to sell Hirschvogel.

The mere memory of all those long winter
evenings, when they had all closed round it, and
roasted chestnuts or crab-apples in it, and listened to the howling of the wind and the deep
sound of the church-bells, and tried very much
to make each other believe that the wolves still
came down from the mountains into the streets
of Hall, and were that very minute growling at
the house door,—all this memory coming on
him with the sound of the city bells.

The knowledge that night drew near upon
him so completely, being added to his hunger
and his fear, so overcame him that he burst out

crying for the fiftieth time since he had been
inside the stove, and felt that he would starve
to death, and wondered dreamily if Hirschvogel
would care.

Yes, he was sure Hirschvogel would care.
Had he not decked it all summer long with
alpine roses and edelweiss and heaths and made
it sweet with thyme and honeysuckle and great
garden-lilies? Had he ever forgotten when Santa
Claus came to make it its crown of holly and ivy
and wreathe it all around?

"Oh, shelter me; save me; take care of me!"
he prayed to the old fire-king, and forgot,
poor little man, that he had come on this wild-
goose chase northward to save and take care of
Hirschvogel!

After a time he dropped asleep, as children
can do when they weep, and little robust hill-
born boys most surely do, be they where they
may.

It was not very cold in this lumber-room;

177

it was tightly shut up, and very full of things,
단단히, 꽉   가득 차다

and at the back of it were the hot pipes of an
                                   뜨거운 관

adjacent house, where a great deal of fuel was
인접한, 가까운   연료, 땔감

burnt.

Moreover, August's clothes were warm ones,
게다가, 더욱이(=in addition)   옷

and his blood was young. So he was not cold,
      피, 혈액

though Munich is terribly cold in the nights of
                지독하게, 혹독하게, 끔찍하게

December; and he slept on and on,—which was
12월   쉬지 않고[계속해서]

a comfort to him, for he forgot his woes, and his
편안함, 안락함, 쾌적함   비통, 비애(=misery)

perils, and his hunger, for a time.
(심각한) 위험

Midnight was once more chiming from all
한밤중, 12시, 자정   한 번 더   울리다, 시간을 알리다

the brazen tongues of the city when he awoke,
놋쇠로 만든   혀, 혓바닥 같이 생긴 것   잠에서 깨다

and, all being still around him, ventured to put
                                   (위험을 무릅쓰고) 감히 ~하다

his head out of the brass door of the stove to see
              밖으로 내밀다

why such a strange bright light was round him.
          이상한   밝은, 눈부신, 빛나는

It was a very strange and brilliant light in-
                이상한, 낯선   훌륭한, 멋진, 눈부신

deed; and yet, what is perhaps still stranger, it
                          아마, 어쩌면

did not frighten or amaze him, nor did what he
      (몹시) 겁먹게 하다   (대단히) 놀라게 하다

saw alarm him either, and yet I think it would
불안하게[두렵게] 만들다(=worry)

have done you or me. For what he saw was

nothing less than all the bric-à-brac in motion.
                        (자그마한) 장식품들   운동, 움직임

178

A big jug, an Apostel-Krug, of Kruessen,
(손잡이가 달린) 주전자[병/항아리/단지]   크로이센
was solemnly dancing a minuet with a plump
근엄하게, 엄숙하게   미뉴에트(우아하고 느린 춤)   통통한
Faenza jar; a tall Dutch clock was going through
파엔차(도자기로 유명한 이탈리아 도시)   시계
a gavotte with a spindle-legged ancient chair; a
가보트(과거 프랑스에서 유행하던 춤)   다리가 가는   고대의, 아주 오래된
very droll porcelain figure of Littenhausen was
우스꽝스러운   자기(磁器)   리텐하우젠
bowing to a very stiff soldier in terre cuite of
절하다, 고개 숙여 인사하다   뻣뻣한   테라코타(점토를 구워 만든 도기)
Ulm.

An old violin of Cremona was playing itself,
크레모나산 바이올린(명품으로 유명)
and a queer little shrill plaintive music that
기묘한, 기이한   새된, 날카로운   애처로운[구슬픈](=mournful)
thought itself merry came from a painted spin-
즐거운, 유쾌한
net covered with faded roses; some gilt Spanish
색 바랜, 희미해진   금박을 입힌
leather had got up on the wall and laughed; a
가죽   벽   웃다
Dresden mirror was tripping about, crowned
드레스덴 ((독일 동부의 도시))   경쾌하게 걸어다니다   왕관을 쓴
with flowers.

A Japanese bonze was riding along on a grif-
일본의   청동상   ~에 올라타다
fin; a slim Venetian rapier had come to blows
날씬한, 가느다란, 얇은   (길고 가느다란) 양날칼
with a stout Ferrara sabre, all about a little pale-
튼튼한, 건장한   군도(날이 휘어져 있는 무거운 검)
faced chit of a damsel in white Nymphenburg
건방진 계집[여자]
china.

A portly Franconian pitcher in grès gris was
약간 뚱뚱한(=stout)   물병
calling aloud.
큰소리로

"Oh, these Italians! always at feud!"

But nobody listened to him at all.

A great number of little Dresden cups and saucers were all skipping and waltzing; the teapots, with their broad round faces, were spinning their own lids like teetotums. The high-backed gilded chairs were having a game of cards together; and a little Saxe poodle, with a blue ribbon at its throat, was running from one to another, whilst a yellow cat of Cornelis Lachtleven's rode about on a Delft horse in blue pottery of 1489.

Meanwhile the brilliant light shed on the scene came from three silver candelabra, though they had no candles set up in them; and, what is the greatest miracle of all, August looked on at these mad freaks and felt no sensation of wonder! He only, as he heard the violin and the spinnet playing, felt an irresistible desire to dance too.

No doubt his face said what he wished; for a

lovely little lady, all in pink and gold and white, with powdered hair, and high-heeled shoes, and all made of the very finest and fairest Meissen china, tripped up to him, and smiled, and gave him her hand, and led him out to a minuet.

And he danced it perfectly,—poor little August in his thick, clumsy shoes, and his thick, clumsy sheepskin jacket, and his rough home-spun linen, and his broad Tyrolean hat!

He must have danced it perfectly, this dance of kings and queens in days when crowns were duly honored, for the lovely lady always smiled benignly and never scolded him at all, and danced so divinely herself to the stately measures the spinnet was playing that August could not take his eyes off her till, their minuet ended, she sat down on her own white-and-gold bracket.

"I am the Princess of Saxe-Royale," she said to him, with a benignant smile; "and you have got through that minuet very fairly."

Then he ventured to say to her,—

"Madame my princess, could you tell me kindly why some of the figures and furniture dance and speak, and some lie up in a corner like lumber? It does make me curious. Is it rude to ask?"

For it greatly puzzled him why, when some of the bric-à-brac was all full of life and motion, some was quite still and had not a single thrill in it.

"My dear child," said the powdered lady, "is it possible that you do not know the reason? Why, those silent, dull things are imitation!" This she said with so much decision that she evidently considered it a condensed but complete answer.

"Imitation?" repeated August, timidly, not understanding.

"Of course! Lies, falsehoods, fabrications!" said the princess in pink shoes, very vivaciously. "They only pretend to be what we are! They never wake up: how can they? No imitation ever had any soul in it yet."

"Oh!" said August, humbly, not even sure that he understood entirely yet.

He looked at Hirschvogel: surely it had a royal soul within it: would it not wake up and speak?

Oh dear! how he longed to hear the voice of his fire-king! And he began to forget that he stood by a lady who sat upon a pedestal of gold-and-white china, with the year 1746 cut on it, and the Meissen mark.

"What will you be when you are a man?" said the little lady, sharply, for her black eyes were quick though her red lips were smiling. "Will you work for the Königliche Porcellan-Manufactur, like my great dead Kandler?"

"I have never thought," said August, stammering; "at least—that is—I do wish—I do hope to be a painter, as was Master Augustin Hirschvogel at Nürnberg."

"Bravo!" said all the real bric-à-brac in one breath, and the two Italian rapiers left off fighting to cry, "Benone!"

For there is not a bit of true bric-à-brac in all Europe that does not know the names of the mighty masters.

August felt quite pleased to have won so much applause, and grew as red as the lady's shoes with bashful contentment.

"I knew all the Hirschvögel, from old Veit downwards," said a fat grès de Flandre beer-jug: "I myself was made at Nürnberg."

And he bowed to the great stove very politely, taking off his own silver hat—I mean lid—with a courtly sweep that he could scarcely have learned from burgomasters.

The stove, however, was silent, and a sickening suspicion (for what is such heart-break as a suspicion of what we love?) came through the mind of August: Was Hirschvogel only imitation?

"No, no, no, no!" he said to himself, stoutly:
though Hirschvogel never stirred, never spoke,
yet would he keep all faith in it.

After all their happy years together, after all
the nights of warmth and joy he owed it, should
he doubt his own friend and hero, whose gilt
lion's feet he had kissed in his babyhood?

"No, no, no, no!" he said, again, with so
much emphasis that the Lady of Meissen looked
sharply again at him.

"No," she said, with pretty disdain; "no, believe me, they may 'pretend' forever. They can
never look like us! They imitate even our marks,
but never can they look like the real thing, never
can they chassent de race."

"How should they?" said a bronze statuette
of Vischer's. "They daub themselves green with
verdigris, or sit out in the rain to get rusted; but
green and rust are not patina; only the ages can
give that!"

"And my imitations are all in primary colors,

185

staring colors, hot as the colors of a hostelry's sign-board!" said the Lady of Meissen, with a shiver.

"Well, there is a grès de Flandre over there, who pretends to be a Hans Kraut, as I am," said the jug with the silver hat, pointing with his handle to a jug that lay prone on its side in a corner. "He has copied me as exactly as it is given to moderns to copy us. Almost he might be mistaken for me. But yet what a difference there is! How crude are his blues! how evidently done over the glaze are his black letters! He has tried to give himself my very twist; but what a lamentable exaggeration of that playful deviation in my lines which in his becomes actual deformity!"

"They carve pear-wood because it is so soft, and dye it brown, and call it me!" said an old oak cabinet, with a chuckle.

"That is not so painful; it does not vulgarize you so much as the cups they paint to-day and

186

christen after me!" said a Carl Theodor cup
이름[명칭]을 붙이다
subdued in hue, yet gorgeous as a jewel.
부드러운, 은은한   빛깔, 색조   아주 멋진, 화려한   보석

"Nothing can be so annoying as to see com-
짜증나는, 성가신
mon gimcracks aping me!" interposed the prin-
싸구려의(=shoddy) 겨우 흉내만 내다(=imitate) 덧붙이다, 끼어들다
cess in the pink shoes.

"They even steal my motto, though it is
훔치다, 도둑질하다 교훈, 격언
Scripture," said a Trauerkrug of Regensburg in
(종교의) 성전[경전]   장례용 항아리
black-and-white.

"And my own dots they put on plain English
(인쇄된 동그란) 점   보통의, 평범한
china creatures!" sighed the little white maid of
한숨 짓다
Nymphenburg.

"That is what is so terrible in these bric-à-
끔찍한, 지독한
brac places," said the princess of Meissen. "It
brings one in contact with such low, imitative
가져오다   닿음, 접촉   낮은   모방하는, 위조된
creatures; one really is safe nowhere nowadays
정말로, 실제로 안전한   요즘에는, 오늘날에는
unless under glass at the Louvre or South Kens-
···이 아닌 한, ···한 경우[때] 외에는   루브르 박물관
ington."

"And they get even there," sighed the grès
심지어, ~조차   한숨 쉬다
de Flandre. "A terrible thing happened to a
플랜더스   끔찍한, 소름끼치는   일어나다, 발생하다
dear friend of mine, a terre cuite of Blasius
테라코타(점토를 구워 만든 도기)
(you know the terres cuites of Blasius date from

1560). Well, he was put under glass in a museum that shall be nameless, and he found himself
set next to his own imitation born and baked
yesterday at Frankfort, and what think you the
miserable creature said to him, with a grin? 'Old
Pipe-clay,'—that is what he called my friend,—
'the fellow that bought me got just as much
commission on me as the fellow that bought
you, and that was all that he thought about. You
know it is only the public money that goes!' And
the horrid creature grinned again till he actually
cracked himself. There is a Providence above all
things, even museums."

"Providence might have interfered before,
and saved the public money," said the little
Meissen lady with the pink shoes.

"After all, does it matter?" said a Dutch jar
of Haarlem. "All the shamming in the world will
not make them us!"

"One does not like to be vulgarized," said the
Lady of Meissen, angrily.

"Ah! if we could all go back to our makers!" (돌아가다 / 제작자, 조물주)

sighed the Gubbio plate (접시), thinking of Giorgio An-dreoli (조르지오 안드레올리) and the glad (기쁜, 고마운) and gracious (자애로운, 품위 있는, 우아한) days of the Renaissance (르네상스 시대): and somehow (왜 그런지 (모르겠지만), 왠지) the words touched (마음을 움직이다, 감동시키다) the frolicsome (즐겁게 뛰노는) souls of the dancing jars, the spinning teapots (찻주전자), the chairs (의자) that were playing cards (카드놀이하다); and the violin stopped its merry (즐거운) music (음악) with a sob (흐느낌), and the spinnet (작은[소형] 피아노) sighed,—thinking of dead hands.

Even (심지어, ~조차) the little Saxe poodle howled (울부짖다) for a master forever (영원히) lost; and only the swords (검, 칼) went on quarrelling (싸움, 다툼), and made such a clattering noise (쨍그랑쨍그랑 시끄러운) that the Japanese bonze (청동상) rode at them on his monster (괴물) and knocked (강타하다, 들이받다) them both (둘 다) right over, and they lay straight and still (곧장, 똑바로), looking foolish (바보 같은, 멍청한), and the little Nymphenburg maid, though she was crying, smiled and almost (거의) laughed.

Then from where the great stove stood there came a solemn (엄숙한, 근엄한) voice. All eyes turned upon (올려다보다) Hirschvogel, and the heart (심장) of its little human comrade (동무, 동지, 동료) gave a great jump of joy.

"My friends," said that clear voice from the turret of Nürnberg faïence, "I have listened to all you have said. There is too much talking among the Mortalities whom one of themselves has called the Windbags. Let not us be like them. I hear among men so much vain speech, so much precious breath and precious time wasted in empty boasts, foolish anger, useless reiteration, blatant argument ignoble mouthings, that I have learned to deem speech a curse, laid on man to weaken and envenom all his undertakings. For over two hundred years I have never spoken myself: you, I hear, are not so reticent. I only speak now because one of you said a beautiful thing that touched me. If we all might but go back to our makers! Ah, yes! if we might! We were made in days when even men were true creatures, and so we, the work of their hands, were true too. We, the begotten of ancient days, derive all the value in us from the fact that our makers wrought at us with zeal, with piety, with

190

integrity, with faith,—not to win fortunes or to glut a market, but to do nobly an honest thing and create for the honor of the Arts and God. I see amidst you a little human thing who loves me, and in his own ignorant childish way loves Art. Now, I want him forever to remember this night and these words; to remember that we are what we are, and precious in the eyes of the world, because centuries ago those who were of single mind and of pure hand so created us, scorning sham and haste and counterfeit. Well do I recollect my master, Augustin Hirschvogel. He led a wise and blameless life, and wrought in loyalty and love, and made his time beautiful thereby, like one of his own rich, many-colored church casements, that told holy tales as the sun streamed through them. Ah, yes, my friends, to go back to our masters!—that would be the best that could befall us. But they are gone, and even the perishable labors of their lives outlive them. For many, many years I, once honored of

진실성, 온전함 · 믿음, 신뢰, 신앙 · 재산, 부; 거금 · 과잉 공급하다 · 고귀하게; 훌륭하게, 당당히 · 창조[창작/창출]하다 · 인간 · 무지한, 무식한; 무학의 · 영원히 · 기억하다 · 귀중한, 값비싼 · 수 세기 · 순수한 · 경멸하다, 멸시하다 · 가짜, 엉터리 · 미워하다, 증오하다 · 위조의, 모조의 · 기억해[생각해] 내다(=recall) · 현명한, 똑똑한 · 떳떳한, 허물 없는 · (변화를) 초래하다 · 충실, 충성 · 그렇게 함으로써, 그것 때문에 · 풍부한 · 여닫이창 · 신성한 · 흐르다, 흘러나오다 · 닥치다 · 가버리다, 사라지다 · 필멸의, 상하기 쉬운

emperors, dwelt in a humble house and warmed in successive winters three generations of little, cold, hungry children. When I warmed them they forgot that they were hungry; they laughed and told tales, and slept at last about my feet. Then I knew that humble as had become my lot it was one that my master would have wished for me, and I was content. Sometimes a tired woman would creep up to me, and smile be-cause she was near me, and point out my golden crown or my ruddy fruit to a baby in her arms. That was better than to stand in a great hall of a great city, cold and empty, even though wise men came to gaze and throngs of fools gaped, passing with flattering words. Where I go now I know not; but since I go from that humble house where they loved me, I shall be sad and alone. They pass so soon,—those fleeting mortal lives! Only we endure,—we, the things that the human brain creates. We can but bless them a little as they glide by: if we have done that,

192

we have done what our masters wished. So in us our masters, being dead, yet may speak and live."

Then the voice sank away in silence, and a strange golden light that had shone on the great stove faded away; so also the light died down in the silver candelabra. A soft, pathetic melody stole gently through the room. It came from the old, old spinnet that was covered with the faded roses.

Then that sad, sighing music of a bygone day died too; the clocks of the city struck six of the morning; day was rising over the Bayerischen-wald.

August awoke with a great start, and found himself lying on the bare bricks of the floor of the chamber, and all the bric-à-brac was lying quite still all around.

The pretty Lady of Meissen was motionless on her porcelain bracket, and the little Saxe poodle was quiet at her side.

He rose slowly to his feet. He was very cold, but he was not sensible of it or of the hunger that was gnawing his little empty entrails. He was absorbed in the wondrous sight, in the wondrous sounds, that he had seen and heard.

All was dark around him. Was it still midnight or had morning come? Morning, surely; for against the barred shutters he heard the tiny song of the robin.

Tramp, tramp, too, came a heavy step up the stair. He had but a moment in which to scramble back into the interior of the great stove, when the door opened and the two dealers entered, bringing burning candles with them to see their way. August was scarcely conscious of danger more than he was of cold or hunger. A marvellous sense of courage, of security, of happiness, was about him, like strong and gentle arms enfolding him and lifting him upwards—upwards—upwards! Hirschvogel would defend him.

천천히 · …을 의식하고[알고] 있는 · 신경을 갉아먹는, 괴롭히는 · 텅 빈 · 내장 · 흡수하다[빨아들이다] · 놀라운, 굉장한 · 광경 · 아직, 여전히 · 확실히, 분명히 · 빗장 걸린 · 아주 작은 · 울새 · (저벅저벅 걷는) 발자국 소리 · 무거운, 묵직한 · 계단 · 순간 · 재빨리 움직이다(=clamber) · 내부, 실내 · (안으로) 들어오다 · 불타고 있는 · 양초, 초 · 거의 …않다 · 의식하는, 자각하는 · 위험 · 추운 · 배고픈, 굶주린 · 놀라운, 믿기 어려운, 초자연적인 · 용기 · 보안, 경비 · 행복 · 강한, 힘 센 · 다정한, 온화한 · 다정하게) 안다(=embrace) · 들어올리다 · 위로 · 방어[수비]하다

The dealers undid the shutters, scaring the
red-breast away, and then tramped about in
their heavy boots and chattered in contented
voices, and began to wrap up the stove once
more in all its straw and hay and cordage.

It never once occurred to them to glance inside. Why should they look inside a stove that
they had bought and were about to sell again for
all its glorious beauty of exterior?

The child still did not feel afraid. A great
exaltation had come to him: he was like one
lifted up by his angels.

Presently the two traders called up their
porters and the stove, heedfully swathed and
wrapped and tended as though it were some
sick prince going on a journey, was borne on the
shoulders of six stout Bavarians down the stairs
and out of the door into the Marienplatz.

Even behind all those wrappings August felt
the icy bite of the intense cold of the outer air at
dawn of a winter's day in Munich.

The men moved the stove with exceed-
ing gentleness and care, so that he had often
been far more roughly shaken in his big broth-
ers' arms than he was in his journey now; and
though both hunger and thirst made themselves
felt, being foes that will take no denial, he was
still in that state of nervous exaltation which
deadens all physical suffering and is at once a
cordial and an opiate. He had heard Hirschvogel
speak; that was enough.

The stout carriers tramped through the city,
six of them, with the Nürnberg fire-castle on
their brawny shoulders, and went right across
Munich to the railway-station, and August in the
dark recognized all the ugly, jangling, pounding,
roaring, hissing railway-noises, and thought,
despite his courage and excitement, "Will it be a
very long journey?"

For his stomach had at times an odd sinking
sensation, and his head sadly often felt light and
swimming.

If it was a very, very long journey he felt half
afraid that he would be dead or something bad
before the end, and Hirschvogel would be so
lonely: that was what he thought most about;
not much about himself, and not much about
Dorothea and the house at home.

He was "high strung to high emprise," and
could not look behind him.

Whether for a long or a short journey, whether for weal or woe, the stove with August still
within it was once more hoisted up into a great
van; but this time it was not all alone, and the
two dealers as well as the six porters were all
with it.

He in his darkness knew that; for he heard
their voices. The train glided away over the Bavarian plain southward; and he heard the men
say something of Berg and the Wurm-See, but
their German was strange to him, and he could
not make out what these names meant.
The train rolled on, with all its fume and

fuss, and roar of steam, and stench of oil and burning coal.

It had to go quietly and slowly on account of the snow which was falling, and which had fallen all night.

"He might have waited till he came to the city," grumbled one man to another. "What weather to stay on at Berg!"

But who he was that stayed on at Berg, August could not make out at all.

Though the men grumbled about the state of the roads and the season, they were hilarious and well content, for they laughed often, and, when they swore, did so good-humoredly, and promised their porters fine presents at New-Year; and August, like a shrewd little boy as he was, who even in the secluded Innthal had learned that money is the chief mover of men's mirth, thought to himself, with a terrible pang,—

"They have sold Hirschvogel for some great sum! They have sold him already!"

198

Then his heart grew faint and sick within
him, for he knew very well that he must soon
die, shut up without food and water thus; and
what new owner of the great fire-palace would
ever permit him to dwell in it?

"Never mind; I will die," thought he; "and
Hirschvogel will know it."

Perhaps you think him a very foolish little
fellow; but I do not.

It is always good to be loyal and ready to
endure to the end.

It is but an hour and a quarter that the train
usually takes to pass from Munich to the Wurm-
See or Lake of Starnberg; but this morning the
journey was much slower, because the way was
encumbered by snow.

When it did reach Possenhofen and stop,
and the Nürnberg stove was lifted out once
more, August could see through the fret-work
of the brass door, as the stove stood upright fac-
ing the lake, that this Wurm-See was a calm and

noble piece of water, of great width, with low
wooded banks and distant mountains, a peace-
ful, serene place, full of rest.

It was now near ten o'clock. The sun had
come forth; there was a clear gray sky here-
abouts; the snow was not falling, though it lay
white and smooth everywhere, down to the
edge of the water, which before long would itself
be ice. Before he had time to get more than a
glimpse of the green gliding surface, the stove
was again lifted up and placed on a large boat
that was in waiting,—one of those very long and
huge boats which the women in these parts use
as laundries, and the men as timber-rafts.

The stove, with much labor and much
expenditure of time and care, was hoisted into
this, and August would have grown sick and
giddy with the heaving and falling if his big
brothers had not long used him to such tossing
about, so that he was as much at ease head, as
feet, downward.

The stove once in it safely with its guardians, the big boat moved across the lake to Leoni. How a little hamlet on a Bavarian lake got that Tuscan-sounding name I cannot tell; but Leoni it is.

The big boat was a long time crossing: the lake here is about three miles broad, and these heavy barges are unwieldy and heavy to move, even though they are towed and tugged at from the shore.

"If we should be too late!" the two dealers muttered to each other, in agitation and alarm. "He said eleven o'clock."

"Who was he?" thought August; "the buyer, of course, of Hirschvogel."

The slow passage across the Wurm-See was accomplished at length: the lake was placid; there was a sweet calm in the air and on the water; there was a great deal of snow in the sky, though the sun was shining and gave a solemn hush to the atmosphere.

Boats and one little steamer were going up
and down; in the clear frosty light the distant
mountains of Zillerthal and the Algau Alps were
visible; market-people, cloaked and furred, went
by on the water or on the banks.

The deep woods of the shores were black and
gray and brown. Poor August could see nothing of a scene that would have delighted him; as
the stove was now set, he could only see the old
worm eaten wood of the huge barge.

Presently they touched the pier at Leoni.

"Now men, for a stout mile and half! You
shall drink your reward at Christmas-time,"
said one of the dealers to his porters, who, stout,
strong men as they were, showed a disposition
to grumble at their task.

Encouraged by large promises, they shoul-
dered sullenly the Nürnberg stove, grumbling
again at its preposterous weight, but little
dreaming that they carried within it a small,
panting, trembling boy; for August began to

tremble now that he was about to see the future (몸을) 떨다, 떨리다 / 미래의, 장래의
owner of Hirschvogel. 주인, 소유자

"If he look a good, kind man," he thought, "I 착한, 좋은 / 친절한, 다정한
will beg him to let me stay with it." 애원하다 / 머물다

The porters began their toilsome journey, 시작하다 / 힘드는, 고생스러운, 고된
and moved off from the village pier. 마을 / 부두

He could see nothing, for the brass door was 놋쇠의, 황동의
over his head, and all that gleamed through it ~위에 / (아주 깨끗하게) 환하다[반짝이다]
was the clear gray sky. 맑은, 깨끗한

He had been tilted on to his back, and if 기울다, (뒤로) 젖혀지다
he had not been a little mountaineer, used to 등산가, 등산객, 산악인
hanging head-downwards over crevasses, and, 매달리다 / 머리를 거꾸로 한 / 빙하의 갈라진 틈
moreover, seasoned to rough treatment by the 게다가, 더욱이 / 거친, 험한 / 대접, 대우
hunters and guides of the hills and the salt- 사냥꾼 / 안내인 / 언덕, 산 / 제염소 일꾼
workers in the town, he would have been made 도시
ill and sick by the bruising and shaking and 아픈 / 아픈, 토할 것 같은 / 멍[흠]이 생기다[생기게 하다], 타박상을 입(히)다
many changes of position to which he had been 변화 / 위치, 자세
subjected. (나쁜 영향을 받아) ~ 되다

The way the men took was a mile and a half

in length, but the road was heavy with snow, 길이는, 길이에 있어서 / 길 / (많은 육체적인 힘을 요하는) 힘든
and the burden they bore was heavier still. 짐 / 더 무거운

The dealers cheered them on, swore at them
~을 격려하다   욕하다
and praised them in one breath; besought them
칭찬하다   간청하다, 애원하다
and reiterated their splendid promises, for a
반복하다, 되풀이하다   화려한, 아주 훌륭한
clock was striking eleven, and they had been
치다 울리다   11시
ordered to reach their destination at that hour,
도착하다   목적지, (물품의) 도착지
and, though the air was so cold, the heat-drops
땀방울
rolled off their foreheads as they walked, they
구르다, 흘러내리다   이마   걸어가다
were so frightened at being late.
두려워하다, 무서워하다

But the porters would not budge a foot
약간 움직이다
quicker than they chose, and as they were not
더 빨리
poor four-footed carriers their employers dared
4발 달린   고용주, 고용인
not thrash them, though most willingly would
(벌로서 매로) 때리다 (=beat)   자진해서, 기꺼이, 쾌히
they have done so.

The road seemed terribly long to the anxious
지독하게, 끔찍하게   불안해하는, 염려하는
tradesmen, to the plodding porters, to the poor
(지쳐서) 터벅터벅 걷다
little man inside the stove, as he kept sinking
내부의, 안의   가라앉다
and rising, sinking and rising, with each of their
올라가다
steps.

Where they were going he had no idea, only
어디로
after a very long time he lost the sense of the
fresh icy wind blowing on his face through the
신선한   얼음처럼 찬   불다

204

brass-work above, and felt by their movements
beneath him that they were mounting steps or
stairs.

Then he heard a great many different voices,
but he could not understand what was being
said. He felt that his bearers paused some time,
then moved on and on again.

Their feet went so softly he thought they
must be moving on carpet, and as he felt a warm
air come to him he concluded that he was in
some heated chambers, for he was a clever little
fellow, and could put two and two together,
though he was so hungry and so thirsty and his
empty stomach felt so strangely.

They must have gone, he thought, through
some very great number of rooms, for they
walked so long on and on, on and on.

At last the stove was set down again, and,
happily for him, set so that his feet were downward.

What he fancied was that he was in some

205

museum, like that which he had seen in the city
of Innspruck.

The voices he heard were very hushed, and
the steps seemed to go away, far away, leaving
him alone with Hirschvogel.

He dared not look out, but he peeped through the brass-work, and all he could see was a big
carved lion's head in ivory, with a gold crown
atop. It belonged to a velvet fauteuil, but he
could not see the chair, only the ivory lion.

There was a delicious fragrance in the air,—a
fragrance as of flowers.

"Only how can it be flowers?" thought August. "It is December!"

From afar off, as it seemed, there came a
dreamy, exquisite music, as sweet as the spinnet's had been, but so much fuller, so much
richer, seeming as though a chorus of angels
were singing all together.

August ceased to think of the museum: he
thought of heaven.

"Are we gone to the Master?" he thought, remembering the words of Hirschvogel.

All was so still around him; there was no sound anywhere except the sound of the far-off choral music. He did not know it, but he was in the royal castle of Berg, and the music he heard was the music of Wagner, who was playing in a distant room some of the motives of "Parsival."

Presently he heard a fresh step near him, and he heard a low voice say, close behind him, "So!"

An exclamation no doubt, he thought, of admiration and wonder at the beauty of Hirschvogel.

Then the same voice said, after a long pause, during which no doubt, as August thought, this new-comer was examining all the details of the wondrous fire-tower.

"It was well bought; it is exceedingly beautiful! It is most undoubtedly the work of Augustin Hirschvogel."

Then the hand of the speaker turned the
round handle of the brass door, and the fainting
soul of the poor little prisoner within grew sick
with fear.

The handle turned, the door was slowly
drawn open, some one bent down and looked in,
and the same voice that he had heard in praise
of its beauty called aloud, in surprise.

"What is this in it? A live child!"

Then August, terrified beyond all self-
control, and dominated by one master-passion,
sprang out of the body of the stove and fell at
the feet of the speaker.

"Oh, let me stay! Pray, meinherr, let me
stay!" he sobbed. "I have come all the way with
Hirschvogel!"

Some gentlemen's hands seized him, not
gently by any means, and their lips angrily muttered in his ear, "Little knave, peace! be quiet!
hold your tongue! It is the king!"

They were about to drag him out of the august atmosphere as if he had been some venomous, dangerous beast come there to slay, but the voice he had heard speak of the stove said, in kind accents, "Poor little child! he is very young. Let him go: let him speak to me."

The word of a king is law to his courtiers: so, sorely against their wish, the angry and astonished chamberlains let August slide out of their grasp, and he stood there in his little rough sheepskin coat and his thick, mud-covered boots, with his curling hair all in a tangle, in the midst of the most beautiful chamber he had ever dreamed of, and in the presence of a young man with a beautiful dark face, and eyes full of dreams and fire; and the young man said to him,—

"My child, how came you here, hidden in this stove? Be not afraid: tell me the truth. I am the king."

August in an instinct of homage cast his
본능, 타고난 소질, 직감　경의, 존경의 표시
great battered black hat with the tarnished
낡은, 닳은　　　　　　　　　흐려지다, 변색되다
gold tassels down on the floor of the room, and
(장식으로 다는) 술　　　　　마루, 바닥
folded his little brown hands in supplication.
접다, 포개다　　　　　　　　　탄원, 애원

He was too intensely in earnest to be in any
열정적으로, 열심히　성실한, 진심 어린
way abashed; he was too lifted out of himself by
창피한, 겸연쩍은　　　…을 들어올리다
his love for Hirschvogel to be conscious of any
의식하는, 자각하는
awe before any earthly majesty.
경외감, 외경심　세속적인　장엄함, 위풍당당함, 폐하, 왕권

He was only so glad—so glad it was the king.
기쁜, 고마운, 반가운
Kings were always kind; so the Tyrolese think,
늘, 언제나, 항상　　티롤 사람들
who love their lords.
왕, 영주

"Oh, dear king!" he said, with trembling
몸을 떨다
entreaty in his faint little voice.
간청, 애원　희미한

"Hirschvogel was ours, and we have loved it
우리의 것
all our lives; and father sold it. And when I saw
팔다
that it did really go from us, then I said to my-
정말로, 실제로
self I would go with it; and I have come all the
way inside it. And last night it spoke and said
~안에, 내부에
beautiful things. And I do pray you to let me live
기도하다, 부탁하다
with it, and I will go out every morning and cut
wood for it and you, if only you will let me stay

beside it. No one ever has fed it with fuel but me since I grew big enough, and it loves me;—it does indeed; it said so last night; and it said that it had been happier with us than if it were in any palace——"

And then his breath failed him, and, as he lifted his little, eager, pale face to the young king's, great tears were falling down his cheeks.

Now, the king likes all poetic and uncommon things, and there was that in the child's face which pleased and touched him. He motioned to his gentlemen to leave the little boy alone.

"What is your name?" he asked him.

"I am August Strehla. My father is Hans Strehla. We live in Hall in the Innthal; and Hirschvogel has been ours so long,—so long!"

His lips quivered with a broken sob.

"And have you truly travelled inside this stove all the way from Tyrol?"

"Yes," said August; "no one thought to look inside till you did."

The king laughed; then another view of the matter occurred to him.

"Who bought the stove of your father?" he inquired.

"Traders of Munich," said August, who did not know that he ought not to have spoken to the king as to a simple citizen, and whose little brain was whirling and spinning dizzily round its one central idea.

"What sum did they pay your father, do you know?" asked the sovereign.

"Two hundred florins," said August, with a great sigh of shame. "It was so much money, and he is so poor, and there are so many of us."

The king turned to his gentlemen-in-waiting.

"Did these dealers of Munich come with the stove."

He was answered in the affirmative.

He desired them to be sought for and brought before him.

As one of his chamberlains hastened on

212

the errand, the monarch looked at August with compassion.

"You are very pale, little fellow: when did you eat last?"

"I had some bread and sausage with me; yesterday afternoon I finished it."

"You would like to eat now?"

"If I might have a little water I would be glad; my throat is very dry."

The king had water and wine brought for him, and cake also; but August, though he drank eagerly, could not swallow anything. His mind was in too great a tumult.

"May I stay with Hirschvogel?—may I stay?" he said, with feverish agitation.

"Wait a little," said the king, and asked, abruptly, "What do you wish to be when you are a man?"

"A painter. I wish to be what Hirschvogel was,—I mean the master that made my Hirschvogel."

213

"I understand," said the king.

Then the two dealers were brought into their sovereign's presence.

They were so terribly alarmed, not being either so innocent or so ignorant as August was, that they were trembling as though they were being led to the slaughter, and they were so utterly astonished too at a child having come all the way from Tyrol in the stove, as a gentleman of the court had just told them this child had done, that they could not tell what to say or where to look, and presented a very foolish aspect indeed.

"Did you buy this Nürnberg stove of this little boy's father for two hundred florins?" the king asked them; and his voice was no longer soft and kind as it had been when addressing the child, but very stern.

"Yes, your majesty," murmured the trembling traders.

"And how much did the gentleman who purchased it for me give to you?"

구입[구매/매입]하다 / 주다

"Two thousand ducats, your majesty," mut-

2,000 / 두카트(과거 유럽에서 사용된 금화)

tered the dealers, frightened out of their wits, and telling the truth in their fright.

무서워하는, 겁 먹은 / 기지, 재치, 지혜 / 진실, 사실 / (섬뜩하게) 놀람, 두려움

The gentleman was not present: he was a trusted counsellor in art matters of the king's, and often made purchases for him.

신하 / 존재하다, 참석하다 / 복심의, 신임 받는 / 상담 전문가, 카운슬러, 조언자 / 자주, 종종 / 구입, 매입, 구매

The king smiled a little, and said nothing.

The gentleman had made out the price to him as eleven thousand ducats.

값, 가격 / 11,000

"You will give at once to this boy's father the two thousand gold ducats that you received, less the two hundred Austrian florins that you paid him," said the king to his humiliated and abject subjects. "You are great rogues. Be thankful you are not more greatly punished."

즉시, 곧장 / 받다 / …을 빼고 / 지불하다 / 굴욕감을 주는 / 극도로 비참한 / (군주국의) 국민, 신하 / 사기꾼, 범죄자(=rascal) / 처벌하다, 벌주다

He dismissed them by a sign to his courtiers, and to one of these gave the mission of making the dealers of the Marienplatz disgorge their ill-gotten gains.

보내다, 물러가게 하다 / 신호 / 시종 / 임무 / 마리엔 광장 / (많은 양을) 쏟아[토해] 내다 / 부정하게 얻은[손에 넣은]

August heard, and felt dazzled yet miserable. Two thousand gold Bavarian ducats for his father! Why, his father would never need to go any more to the salt-baking! And yet, whether for ducats or for florins, Hirschvogel was sold just the same, and would the king let him stay with it?—would he?

"Oh, do! oh, please do!" he murmured, joining his little brown weather-stained hands, and kneeling down before the young monarch, who himself stood absorbed in painful thought, for the deception so basely practised for the greedy sake of gain on him by a trusted counsellor was bitter to him.

He looked down on the child, and as he did so smiled once more.

"Rise up, my little man," he said, in a kind voice; "kneel only to your God. Will I let you stay with your Hirschvogel? Yes, I will; you shall stay at my court, and you shall be taught to be a painter,—in oils or on porcelain as you will,—

and you must grow up worthily, and win all the
가치 있게, 훌륭하게.
laurels at our Schools of Art, and if when you
(영예의 상징으로서의) 월계관
are twenty-one years old you have done well
21세
and bravely, then I will give you your Nürnberg
용감하게, 훌륭하게
stove, or, if I am no more living, then those who
reign after me shall do so. And now go away
(국왕이) 다스리다[통치하다]
with this gentleman, and be not afraid, and you
shall light a fire every morning in Hirschvo-
불을 피우다
gel, but you will not need to go out and cut the
wood."

Then he smiled and stretched out his hand;
(팔다리를) 뻗다[뻗치다]
the courtiers tried to make August understand
조신, 신하   시도하다
that he ought to bow and touch it with his lips,
(마땅히) ~해야 하다
but August could not understand that anyhow;
he was too happy.
행복한
He threw his two arms about the king's
던지다
knees, and kissed his feet passionately; then
열렬히, 격렬하게
he lost all sense of where he was, and fainted
정신을 잃다, 기절하다
away from hunger, and tire, and emotion, and
굶주림   피로   감정
wondrous joy.
경이로운, 경탄스러운(=wonderful)

As the darkness of his swoon closed in
on him, he heard in his fancy the voice from
Hirschvogel saying,—

"Let us be worthy our maker!"

He is only a scholar yet, but he is a happy
scholar, and promises to be a great man.

Sometimes he goes back for a few days to
Hall, where the gold ducats have made his father prosperous.

In the old house-room there is a large white
porcelain stove of Munich, the king's gift to
Dorothea and 'Gilda.

And August never goes home without going
into the great church and saying his thanks to
God, who blessed his strange winter's journey in
the Nürnberg stove.

As for his dream in the dealers' room that
night, he will never admit that he did dream it;
he still declares that he saw it all, and heard the
voice of Hirschvogel.

And who shall say that he did not? for what
is the gift of the poet and the artist except to see
재능, 재주   시인   예술가
the sights which others cannot see and to hear
(눈에 보이는) 광경[모습]
the sounds that others cannot hear?
              다른 사람들

🐾 나만의 리뷰 *and* 명문장

📚 나만의 리뷰 *and* 명문장

📖 나만의 리뷰 *and* 명문장